A New Approach to Procreative Ethics

Chapter 1
What's Wrong with Procreation?

Some of the inconvenient facts

In Western societies, anywhere from 70% to 90% of people will have children at some point in their lives. This is an overwhelming majority of men and women.

It's also, in itself, not a topic that's very much discussed publicly. Sure, we discuss the impact of having children, especially on women's lives and careers. We also discuss the impact of having children on relationships. And that gives us some pretty interesting results.

As it turns out, having children has a profound negative impact on families: it's correlated with lower happiness, life satisfaction, marital satisfaction, and mental well-being. As it's popularly said, it destroys your sex life. It also keeps divorce levels lower, because people who don't get along are forced to stay together "because of the children." It's no wonder that a third of parents say they regret their decision of having children.

Pregnancies also come with their own problems, ranging from constipation, gas, vaginal secretions, and getting kicking by the fetus, to serious psychiatric problems (women who give birth have a

72% greater incidence of psychiatric problems than before giving birth, while abortion carries no significant risk), and medical complications and death (rare occurrences in the Western world, but a significant risk in Third World countries).

There are not only personal consequences to procreation, but also global, planetary consequences. Each new human being born in the Western world adds a burden of pollution that we all pay for, anywhere from 5 to 20 tons of CO_2 per year. It also adds to the torture and killing of livestock, to the tune of 30 to 150 kg per year. Producing the manufactured goods required for the life of that human being also entails hard labor, including slave labor. More than 18 million slaves are involved in producing goods like clothing, electronics, food, and so on, which end up on our shelves.

The reasons given for procreation

These are all serious repercussions that should give us pause, but people seem to procreate without giving much thought, if any, to these consequences. This in itself is a rather interesting fact. While I don't want to stereotype parents, it seems like parents generally give less thought to their reasons for having children as they would buying a car or a house, even though these latter purchases have less of a financial and personal impact on people than having a child.

The reasons parents give for having children are varied, but they have certain common themes. Here are some randomly sampled examples:

> I had children because I wanted children, and I thought I'd be a good parent. I have always imagined myself raising children. I love babies and children...

> I always wanted to be a mommy, among other things. There was my gymnast phase, my ballerina phase, my scientist phase. But the constant was a baby doll.

> I had children because I wanted a family. In my culture, we stay together and help each other grow. Again, it's my upbringing and I embrace it.

> I had kids because I fundamentally enjoy the family dynamic, and because I knew I had a lot of good shit to teach young people.

> I had children because I wanted children. I wanted the love, closeness and chaos that comes with offspring.

> To be honest, it started when my husband and I just reached a point where we threw up our hands and said: Why not give this a shot and see what happens?

> I had children because I want to be a parent, and I want to be there for them.

These answers give us a good idea of the range of reasons for procreation: socialization (gender socialization, cultural socialization), conformity (wanting a family, wanting to be a parent, "giving it a shot"), and personal needs (need for love and closeness, need to be a parent).

These are not the only reasons, of course, but the other ones aren't much better. For example, there is the "biological clock" which people use to rationalize their desire for procreation. It's very convenient to have a supposed biological process to back up what you're saying, but there is zero scientific evidence of a connection between hormone levels, or some other biological factor, and the desire to procreate. Laura Carroll, author of The Baby Matrix, has opined that the idea that procreating is instinctual makes no sense because, if that was the case, there'd be no need for social pressure:

> In addition to pushing the idea that parenthood was "the" path to fulfillment in life, another had to do with the idea that "normal" women experience an instinctual longing from within to have a child, and if they didn't there was something wrong with them. This belief is part of the larger pronatal "Destiny Assumption" that was created many years ago, that, like the Fulfillment Assumption, has stuck long after its usefulness.

> The deep feelings of wanting to have a child have their roots in a learned desire from strong, long-standing social and cultural pronatal influences -- not biological ones. And we've been influenced so strongly for so long that it just feels "innate."

What she calls the "Destiny Assumption" is this belief that we are biologically wired to want to have children. Personally, I would go further and say it's a mass delusion. Either way, it's got nothing to do with biology and more to do with ideology.

Another common reason is the desire to propagate one's genes or the family line. Procreation is not a particularly good way of spreading your genes, unless you don't mind mixing them with someone else's (cloning would be more far more accurate than sexual reproduction, anyway). Either way, they are both based on the expectation of one's genes or family continuing to exist in the future, but there is no particular reason for this expectation to exist. We are not our genes or our family.

I will skip over the more trivial reasons related to racism ("we have to breed more than THEM!") and religion ("God said to be fruitful and multiply"), as they are unlikely to convince anyone who doesn't already buy into the worldview they're a part of.

What all these answers have in common is that they are all about the parent: the parent's needs, the parent's socialization, the parent's expectations. This is not surprising. After all, a parent could hardly be procreating in the name of a child's values, when that child is not even born yet. All reasons for procreating are necessarily selfish.

Parents reading this may start objecting at this point. After all, I've already listed a number of negative consequences that procreation brings to relationships and to women. How can a selfish act be so dangerous to the individual? We think of a selfish act as being an "easy way out," and having children is certainly not an "easy way out." It's a great deal of hard work that comes with a great number of risks.

As I already mentioned, I don't think most people even think about these risks when they take the decision of procreating. But that fact alone does not make it a selfish act, merely an extremely imprudent one.

Children: the missing corner

So far I have only discussed the consequences to the parents and to society. We are very familiar with these kinds of consequences, because parents have some interest in them (usually only after they have a child and start feeling said consequences). In order to get the full picture on the ethics of procreation, we must include the corner of the procreative triangle that never gets discussed and which necessarily remains silent: the child.

This book aims to bring to bear this new child-centered perspective to the issue of procreative ethics (whether it is right or wrong to procreate, and in what contexts). It is based on the premise that existing perspectives on procreative ethics must take into account two ideologies in particular:

Childism: The awareness that we live in profoundly childist societies, i.e. societies where children are seen as inferior or not fully human, and that this prejudice provides powerful support for procreation and parenting.

Antinatalism: The ethical position that procreation (within the scope of this book, human procreation specifically) is wrong.

These two ideologies, thus summarized, may seem implausible on their face. The reaction of most people, when confronted to them, is incredulity. This is a natural reaction, as procreation is considered normal and part of a successful life. There is a sort of standard life blueprint (what Laura Carroll calls the Fulfillment Assumption) which we're all indoctrinated to believe is the way to have a successful life: go to college, get a career, get married, buy a house, have children, retire, have grandchildren (not necessarily in that order).

Because of this, any ideology which argues against procreation will inevitably appear implausible. If having children is necessary to have a successful life, then not wanting to have children, let alone being against having children, must be an aberration. Childfree people are very well aware of their social status: although we tolerate people who don't have children due to sterility or loneliness, childfreedom is not a popular stance.

But a further problem with the life blueprint is that it objectifies children: children are not human beings but a thing (like marriage or a house), a prize, that you must collect in order to get to the next level, like levels or points in a video game. Within that mindset, procreation is justified solely by the values and desires of the parents, and the values and desires of the future child do not, and cannot, be included (because, again, the future child's values and desires do not yet exist).

The quotes I listed earlier reflects this objectification. Children are not seen as ends in themselves but as means to some other end: the end of receiving love and attention, the end of fulfilling one's socialization, the end of gaining social status as a parent or teacher, and so on.

In philosophy, the term "end" designates the ultimate goal of an action, and the term "means" designates actions or objects which are used towards that ultimate goal. When we say a person is a means to an end, we are saying that the person is being used to fulfill some goal which is not connected to that person's values or desires. When we say that a person is an end in themselves, we mean that the person is seen as innately valuable.

Sociopaths and authoritarians generally regard other human beings as means to an end. When making decisions about how to treat others, they think not of how to get people on their side and come to some mutual understanding, but rather of how they can exploit people to accomplish some objective. They see other people as gullible fools, as tools that must be exploited, like we would use any other tool to fulfill a goal. Objectification goes hand in hand with treating people as means to an end.

The principle that we should not treat people as means to an end is, I think, pretty fundamental. All societies have rules against things like murder, theft, and so on, actions which people undertake in defiance of the victims' interests or desires. All tyrannies, all slavery, all war, all attacks against human rights crucially involve treating people as means to an end (and, generally, objectification and dehumanization as well).

As I will explain in detail later, the perspective that concerns us here, that of the child, entails the awareness that children are being treated, not as full human beings, but as means to an end. Antinatalism brings us to the conclusion that the act of procreation itself requires us to see children not as human beings but as means to an end, something which we find unacceptable (at least in theory) when applied to anyone else. Childism brings us to the conclusion that procreation is part of a clear and definable pattern of prejudice deployed against children, a pattern which involves treating children as means to some end. Antinatalism and childism are linked together, because both are directly concerned with exposing the missing side of the procreative equation, that of children.

Now you might say that parents are concerned with their children's welfare and want the best for them. I don't dispute the fact that many parents (not all of them, obviously, but many) are concerned with their children's welfare and want the best for them.

In this neo-liberalist and post-modernist age, it has become fashionable to reduce all criticism of institutions or ideologies, i.e. systemic criticism, to criticism of individual choice. Popular debates on capitalism are now often about whether workers or business owners are making the right decisions, and popular debates on feminism are diverted to the issue of whether women are living the right lifestyle and holding the correct opinions.

But systemic criticism really has nothing to do with blaming individuals. Individuals generally have good intentions but they are still part of a society which contains within it institutions and beliefs which motivate them to act in certain ways. It is those institutions and beliefs that are the problem, not the individuals. When I talk about procreation being wrong or about children being used as means to an end, I am talking about structures of oppression that are spread throughout entire societies, not about any specific parent doing "bad things" or making "bad choices."

A standard reply to systemic criticism is that any problems are the result of the actions of a few "bad apples" who spoil the rest of the barrel. Sure, people can point to specific parents who do particularly egregious things, such as have twelve children, or kill their child because they followed a book that advocated strict corporal punishment. But concentrating the discussion on those cases erases the very real incentives that motivates all parents in our societies, not just the "bad" ones.

Just to be clear, I am glad that many parents have their children's best interests at heart. Abusive or manipulative parents are always undesirable. Those conversations are happening, and that's a good thing. But we also need to look at the big picture, at the way we glorify procreation in our societies, how illogical and childist it all really is, and those conversations are not yet happening.

Justifications for natalism

There is already a name for the pro-procreation ideology, and that's *natalism* (with *antinatalism* being the obvious counterpoint). The support for population growth is always defended in terms of economic growth and progress. We are constantly told that we need bigger populations to take care of the older generations, to solve the problems left behind by those older generations, to keep the economy growing, and so on.

For example, economist Bryan Caplan, currently the most visible proponent of natalism in the United States, explains:

People—especially smart, creative people—are the source of new ideas. Imagine deleting half the names in your music collection—or half the visionaries in the computer industry. Think how much poorer the world would be. But population doesn't merely increase the supply of new ideas. It increases the demand as well. Suppose an idea is worth $1 per person, but takes a decade to develop. On an island with a hundred inhabitants, the idea would remain undiscovered; inventors are better off picking coconuts. But in a world with seven billion customers, inventors scramble to bring the new idea to market...

Population also enriches us in a more immediate way. Despite constant complaints about cities' crowds and congestion, city folk gladly pay higher urban rents. Even introverts and outright misanthropes shell out massive premiums to live near millions of strangers. What are they after? The obvious answer is choices—choices about where to work, what to buy, how to play, and who to meet. These choices, like ideas, come from people—suppliers who offer them, and demanders [sic] who sustain them. When population goes up, everyone gets extra choices.

In the light of what I've written above, I think you can see the main flaw in this line of reasoning: it is all based on the assumption that children are means to an end. It doesn't matter to Caplan what future children might or might not want for their lives, they must be brought into this world specifically so they can become avid consumers, suppliers of goods for "city folk," or visionaries. To him, that's a good enough reason to bring more children into this world.

In his book L'Art de Guillotiner les Procréateurs[1], Théophile de Giraud makes a similar objection:

> The political discourse vaunts procreation for economic aims: we must make more children to guarantee pensions for the next decades, to rejuvenate the aging workforce, to prevent a dangerous reversal of the age distribution, or to sustain industrial growth, etc.
>
> So many emetics that are knocked about regularly in the mass media.
>
> This is then the theme of the child as wealth-giver: it goes without saying that this argument for procreation as prosperity contradicts the minimum requirements of Ethics, since it is founded on the objectification of the Other, that is to say, the principle of slavery…
>
> We procreate sometimes because of a need, sometimes for pleasure. The former is nothing more than slavery, the latter sadism, but whatever the reason, we only procreate

from absolute selfishness! The child is never conceived as an end but always as a means, which is purely machiavellian!

Also, consider that all these benefits of procreation that Caplan lists can be achieved in a perfectly ethical way: by giving more opportunities to the billions of people already living on this planet. There are a lot of people in this world who can't become singers, innovators, or producers, simply because they haven't had the education or opportunities necessary to even have those possibilities. This is in large part due to the capitalist system we operate under, where education and opportunities are basically apportioned on the basis of how much your parents can afford.

But the connection with capitalism is much deeper. Capitalism is predicated on, and wholly depends upon, constant, never-ending growth. This desperate process can only be driven by two things: finding more efficient ways to generate production or consumption from the people already existing (usually by forcibly lowering wages or work conditions, or massive advertising campaigns), or creating more people who will produce and consume. Because of this, procreation, immigration, and anything else that raises population is vital for the survival of capitalism (and baby items alone are an industry worth billions of dollars, making them inextricably tied to the capitalist system as a whole).

We know that children are means to an end for the parents. All the more true is this principle for

14

nation-states. New people are a new labor force. New people are new consumers. New people are new workers. New people are new voters. And for imperialist nations, new people are bodies to sacrifice. The nation did not promote your birth, and the birth of millions of others, because it cares about your personality, your skills or your intelligence. The nation promoted your birth because you are a tool through which it can bolster its power.

Even if we accept that children should be means to some end, and that the best ends are economic growth and innovation, producing more children under such a system would only mean that some percentage of them would be discarded by the system and thus become useless means for their assigned ends. Taking care of the children we already have, on the other hand, would be a much more efficient way of fulfilling those ends. But an even better strategy would be to treat children like human beings, and try to ensure their well-being and happiness instead of treating them like tools.

And what is Caplan's answer if these future people are unhappy and don't want to fulfill their assigned roles as economy-growers and innovators? Well, they can just kill themselves. Natalists call this the "free disposal" argument; bizarrely, they believe that suicide is "cheap and easy," and that therefore everyone on Earth wants to be there. Never mind the fact that the vast majority of suicides end in failure, and that there are many valid reasons why someone might not want to kill themselves (and never mind the social costs, too). That's how highly they value the well-being of anyone who isn't them.

The only cogent argument I've heard against the erasure of children in natalism is that we should not take future children into account because they are not yet alive, and it makes no sense to talk about people who are not born yet. I will analyze this response when I discuss the Non-Identity Problem in chapter 6.

As incredibly callous as their attitude towards new people is, we must also keep in mind that mothers are also a means to an end in the natalist argument. There is no discussion of what women might want to be doing rather than having children: it is merely assumed that, whatever the number of new children that "we" (the nation-state) need, there will be women present and willing to provide wombs. A woman is an abstraction that produces children for the good of society, for the good of "the economy," or for the good of the State. It really does not matter at all how many women's lives are turned upside down or ruined in the process.

So there seems to be a pretty strong link between natalism, which is founded on the objectification of women and children, and anti-feminism, which also promotes the objectification of women. For one thing, natalism provides the theoretical justification for anti-feminism. The reasoning goes something like this:

1. Women are sexual objects... (anti-feminism)
2. ... because they were made that way by

God/nature... (genderism)
3. ... because the survival of the species demands it. (natalism)

We don't usually observe this kind of objectification in other political issues. When we talk about the draft, moral issues immediately come up: the draft is a form of slave labor, the draft is justified by utilitarian rhetoric and that's wrong, and so on. When we talk about the war on drugs, again we talk about moral issues such as civil rights, the harm caused by police repression or by drugs, and so on. We talk endlessly about whether immigrants or the poor are "deserving" or "undeserving," and a lot of political activism revolves around the moral judgments we pass over other people based on the stories politicians and the media tell us about them.

But when we talk about procreation, the moral arguments are curiously absent. Natalists do not argue that procreation is morally right, whether parents are worthy, or the harms of existence, they argue instead that increased procreation is practical and convenient. This is very strange indeed, although the fact that the objectification of women is commonplace may be an explanation. Because we routinely ignore the values and desires of women and children, considering either of those categories of people when discussing public policy simply does not cross people's minds (even though together they compose a majority of the population).

And yet there are so few people who question the

natalist imperative. Those who do question it receive little more than platitudes like "life is precious" or "life is a gift." Life may be a gift, but if so, it is a gift in the same sense than giving someone the flu is a gift. As for being precious, well, one must ask: precious for who? There are plenty of people who don't believe that their life is precious at all, including, for example, the 800 000 people who kill themselves around the world every year.

These sayings are not adequate answers to the profound problems of natalism. But when they are applied to issues like suicide and abortion, they are downright criminal. Granted, suicide is not directly a procreative issue, but it does have some bearing on the issue of whether life is good enough to bring more people into it (a subject which I will discuss in chapter 5); abortion is much more relevant.

Obviously people who consider suicide or abortion have good reason to believe that life would not be a gift, at least in their particular case. So simply repeating the same thing again is not an adequate response, it's just intimidation. A lot of the antinatalist arguments I'll discuss in this book will concern this assertion that "life is a gift" and that "life is precious." For now, all I will say is that they are superficial and vacuous.

Apart from those statements, there is another special form of argument used to rationalize natalism, which I've already touched upon above: the so-called evolutionary mandate to survive and reproduce. This argument is mostly used by secular liberals who have failed to understand anything from the now discredited field of Social Darwinism: a *description* of the process of "survival of the species" cannot simply be turned into a *prescription* of how people's lives or societies should be run, unless further argument is presented to bridge the two. Just like the existence of "survival of the fittest" (which does not solely mean "a ruthless competition that weeds out the weak") does not prove the need for eugenics, the fact that species must procreate in order to survive does not prove that humans must procreate, let alone that all humans must procreate, in order to be "evolutionary winners."

The evolutionary mandate nonsense finds its fullest expression in the pseudo-science of evolutionary psychology and its predecessor, sociobiology, which assume that all sexual behaviors, including rape and husbands killing their spouses for believing they're cheating on them, are validated by evolutionary theory. Here is an example, from Applied Evolutionary Psychology, edited by S. Craig Roberts:

> ...[T]he basic concepts of natural selection, reproductive success, and sexual selection have given rise to two evolutionary theories of rape behaviour. The first theory postulates that rape is a direct adaptation, in that a condition-dependent predisposition to rape behaviour in certain conditions has a net positive effect on a male's reproductive success in the human evolutionary

> environment (Thornhill 1999; Thornhill and Palmer 2000)... The second theory of rape views the behavioural tendency to rape as a by-product of adaptive behaviours related to male sexual strategy (Thornhill and Palmer 2000). For example, rape could be a by-product of an adaptive male tendency to aggressively pursue willing sexual partners...
>
> Jones notes that these theories of rape implicate male sexual strategies (however unconsciously). This is a departure from prevailing social science theories of rape that focus on male aggression and violence towards women (Thornhill and Palmer 2000).

Now, I'm sure most people who argue for the evolutionary mandate wouldn't agree with this nonsense soup, and I certainly don't mean to say that any of them support rape. But if we accept the argument that reproduction is our "evolutionary duty," then it's hard to see how one would reject the argument that rape is a man's "evolutionary duty." Both are based on a vastly oversimplified reading of evolution as "survival of the fittest" and the unjustified belief that any principle which one can derive from that (be it either "reproduction is the measure of evolutionary success" or "rape is a direct adaptation") must be applied to human actions.[2]

Related to this, people also make the claim that we

have a procreative instinct, as proven by the "biological clock." I've already make my case against that concept. But the idea of a procreative instinct is not much more logical: if we really had a procreative instinct, then the advent of health care technologies, fertility treatments, artificial reproduction, and so on, should have made birth rates skyrocket. Instead, we observe the exact opposite phenomenon.

We can make comparisons with some other desires that we know are actually instinctual. For example, humans crave fat and sugar. The more food technology we have, the more we're able to produce foodstuffs with a variety of fats and sugars, and this has led to higher levels of obesity, not to general emaciation. If you think the latter possibility is absurd, then you should see the belief in a procreative instinct as being equally absurd.

Another problem with the notion of a procreative instinct is that we are subjected, from the youngest age, to gender-based propaganda. Girls specifically are subjected to propaganda portraying them as "nurturing," as meant to have children, that they should play with dolls, that motherhood is a great thing. As adults, we're given financial incentives to procreate, and, as any childfree couple could tell you, there's great social pressure to have children. Some countries have even run ad campaigns to encourage procreation!

If we really had a procreative instinct, why would we need all this propaganda and all these incentives to get people to procreate? Again, think of other instincts and try to apply them to this situation, and it's pretty ridiculous. Can you imagine an ad campaign telling people to eat? (Calories: the new white meat!) An ad campaign telling people to have sex (protected sex, obviously, otherwise it would just be another campaign for procreation)? An ad campaign telling people to sleep? (You gotta lie down/ho-ri-zon-ta-lly/e-ve-ry niiiiight!)

Finally, it is clear to anyone who looks at the way humans are built sexually that procreation cannot be the end goal of our anatomy. For one thing, it is now common knowledge that the female sex drive is highest after 40 years old, when women generally either cannot have children or need fertility treatment, and when having children entails a higher risk of complications. Furthermore, sexual pleasure in both men and women do not correlate with procreation: the clitoris has the highest concentration of nerves of all human sex organs, yet has no procreative role, and the male prostate gland gives sexual pleasure despite such an act having no role in procreation. Finally, even the one act of sexual pleasure that is involved in procreation, ejaculation, can equally well be done through masturbation, which is definitely not procreative (unless you're using some form of artificial insemination, but that can't possibly have anything to do with an organism that evolved without such technology).

No, I think it's obvious that, if there is any instinct at work here, it could only be a sexual instinct (although, due to the existence of asexuals, even that is doubtful) We've bought into the association between sex and procreation because birth control was banned by the Catholic Church, and having sex always entailed the risk of procreation. There is no particular need for this association to hold true: to have children one must have sex (barring artificial means), but sex does not have to entail the risk of procreation (such as in the case of vasectomies and female sterilizations, much maligned operations due to the lack of procreative ethics in our societies).

Procreation is part of the natural order, but so is cancer (there is more to say about this analogy, and I will get back to it at a later time). It's rather interesting to me that the same seculars who push the procreation and "life is a gift" lines are also the ones who are most likely to fully apprehend the cruelty of nature, because of their scientific inclinations. Richard Dawkins, a biologist who is famous for his atheistic position, has this to say about nature in his book River Out of Eden:

> The total amount of suffering per year in the natural world is beyond all decent contemplation. During the minute that it takes me to compose this sentence, thousands of animals are being eaten alive, many others are running for their lives, whimpering with fear, others are slowly being devoured from within by rasping parasites, thousands of all kinds are dying of starvation, thirst, and disease. It must be so. If there ever is a time of plenty, this very

fact will automatically lead to an increase in the population until the natural state of starvation and misery is restored. In a universe of electrons and selfish genes, blind physical forces and genetic replication, some people are going to get hurt, other people are going to get lucky, and you won't find any rhyme or reason in it, nor any justice.

A pretty bleak view of nature compared to the usual pablum we hear about the natural world, but an accurate one. Certainly there is much that people find praiseworthy in nature, but the facts presented by Dawkins remain true regardless.

But then we get this sort of natalist propaganda from the same Dawkins in his book Unweaving the Rainbow:

> We are going to die, and that makes us the lucky ones. Most people are never going to die because they are never going to be born. The potential people who could have been here in my place but who will in fact never see the light of day outnumber the sand grains of Arabia. Certainly those unborn ghosts include greater poets than Keats, scientists greater than Newton. We know this because the set of possible people allowed by our DNA so massively exceeds the set of actual people. In the teeth of these stupefying odds it is you and I, in our ordinariness, that are here... I am lucky to be alive and so are you...

> We are so staggeringly lucky to find ourselves in the spotlight. However brief our time in the sun, if we waste a second of it, or complain that it is dull and barren or (like a child) boring, couldn't this be seen as a callous insult to those unborn trillions who will never be offered life in the first place?

How can we reconcile the keen awareness of suffering in this world displayed by the first quote with the starry-eyed optimism of the second quote? Sure, the quotes belong to different books, and as such serve a different role in each case. But seen as two different beliefs held by the same person, they don't make a lot of sense: we are lucky to having been born, against stupefying odds, in a world where the amount of suffering is beyond our ability to imagine. That doesn't sound lucky at all!

What's going on here is probably some form of compartmentalization. This concept is already well understood in the case of scientists who also hold to a religious dogma; they put their religious beliefs and their scientific beliefs in different compartments, to be opened at different times: scientific beliefs opened at work, religious beliefs opened at home or at church.

But there's no reason why this principle cannot apply to secular scientists as well. A biologist like Dawkins has to ignore what he knows about the cruelty of nature, at least if he wishes to remain in the mainstream regarding procreation and the glory

25

of being alive (instead of being a crackpot like me).

Furthermore, as David Benatar (a professor of philosophy who I will come back to, as he's an important figure in antinatalism) points out, the flaws in Dawkins' reasoning should be fairly obvious to anyone well versed in evolutionary theory:

> There are well-established features of human psychology that lead most people to underestimate how bad the quality of their lives is. Chief among these psychological features is 'pollyannaism', an inclination most people have towards optimism. Research has shown, for example, that people selectively recall the good more often than the bad, overestimate how well things will go, and tend to think that the quality of their life is above average.
>
> It is curious that Professor Dawkins seems so unaware of these optimistic biases, given their obvious evolutionary explanation. Those with the right dose of delusion are more likely to produce offspring, whereas those who see the human condition for what it is, are unlikely to want to reproduce it. Optimistic delusions, within a normal human range, are thus adaptive. The delusions that help people cope with the human predicament are often theistic, but they are not always so. Professor Dawkins is quick to debunk the theistic consolations and

to begrudge those who seek comfort in them. Yet he does not cast the same critical light on his own delusions and consolations.

Using evolution as an argument in favor of procreation, or as the basis of any other moral judgment, is nonsense. Evolution is a purposeless, undirected process. DNA molecules do not seek anything. The belief that evolution exists for the sake of, and is driven by, gene replication (and thus, reproduction) is a metaphor that helps understand how evolution works, but it is not a statement of fact. In reality, evolution does not exist for the sake of anything, and it doesn't pursue anything; it is no less mechanistic than the law of gravity, the laws of thermodynamics, or capillary action. Evolution does not give purpose to humans any more than gravity gives a purpose to the Sun or capillary action gives a purpose to straws.

Dawkins wants to sell books, and books which argue that life is a raw deal and that procreation is undesirable do not sell (I don't exactly expect this work to become a bestseller either). So, even if he could make the connection between suffering in nature and the undesirability of life, he would be better off not writing about it.

For similar reasons, it's undesirable for anyone who's in a position to be heard to openly discuss such topics. There's little incentive for people to publicly declare that life is meaningless, that procreation is undesirable, or that breeders are selfish, especially since most people are breeders and are likely to get angry at such talk. The positions and arguments I discuss in this book are unlikely to enter the public consciousness, unless there is an incredible shift in public opinion.

Some see this fact in itself as an argument for procreation: any view opposing procreation is *prima facie* extremely counter-intuitive, or even *prima facie* absurd, that we shouldn't even bother examining it at all.

But this is a bad argument. For millennia people would have said that the view that women should be equal to men is *prima facie* absurd: they could observe the "obvious inferiority" of women in their own societies, although now we know that it was nothing but bigotry backed by self-fulfilling prophecies, confirmation bias, and the effect of stereotype threat, amongst other things.

Likewise, slavery was accepted as the way of the world for millennia, and any scholar could have told you that any hypothetical anti-slavery view was counter-intuitive. Nowadays, we accept the arguments against slavery as valid, and there's nothing counter-intuitive about them any more.

Granted, this is not an argument in favor of my view, or anyone else's view, but it is an argument I put forward to prove that you should not reject any anti-procreation view simply because it is anti-procreation. The fact that procreation is an accepted view does not explain away the major ethical and logical flaws I've discussed in this chapter:

1. There are many serious reasons not to procreate, and those reasons are not openly discussed.
2. All reasons commonly put forward for having children are selfish.
3. Natalism entails treating children and women as means to an end, which is an unethical stance.
4. The common arguments put forward to justify natalism are not credible.

Natalism is a simplistic, dehumanizing, objectifying ideology which serves the interests of those in power but fails to address even the most minimal ethical issues such as consent and reciprocity (i.e. Golden Rule-type principles).

Whatever your position on procreation, you must admit that these points beg for a much, much deeper kind of discussion on the topic than what we've seen so far.

The rest of this book

So far, I have kept the discussion in the general terms of procreation and natalism, and I have not discussed any arguments against procreation as such. The rest of this book will delve into the core of the issue.

Chapter 2 is, as titled, a small digression on the subject of ethics. I thought it would be appropriate to address basic issues of ethics before I get further into ethical arguments.

Chapter 3 defines two concepts which I think are crucial to understanding childism, the alignment paradigm and the domestication hierarchy.

Chapter 4 defines childism and looks at the basic reasoning used to justify childism.

Chapter 5 introduces antinatalism, as well as some of the major arguments for it.

Chapter 6 continues the exploration of antinatalist arguments, with the aim of answering possible objections to antinatalism in general.

Chapter 7 goes into the consequence of childism and antinatalism for the anti-abortion and pro-choice positions.

Chapter 8 presents the major consequences that childist prejudice has on children around the world.

Chapter 9 ends with what is perhaps the most commonly asked question, "what's the solution?"

Chapter 2
A Small Digression on the Subject of Ethics

I've put a lot of emphasis on the ethical principle that we should not treat others as means to an end or, as formulated in philosophy, that we should treat others as ends-in-themselves.

The most famous formulation of treating others as ends-in-themselves was written by philosopher Immanuel Kant:

> Act in such a way that you treat humanity, whether in your own person or in the person of any other, never merely as a means to an end, but always at the same time as an end.

To Kant, this was one of the fundamental principles of ethics. We may treat objects like objects, as that is precisely what they are. But humans, like you and me, have the capacity to value and reason, and therefore should not be treated like objects.

One obvious reason why this is true is because no one's values are inherently superior to anyone else's. This is why, for instance, we dislike dictators: there is no clear reason why one person's values or well-being should have priority over that of millions of people. The concept of fairness, that we should deal with each other as equals, is universal and has also been observed in other primate species.[3] No logical argument has ever successfully proven that we should care more about one person's values than another.[4]

A common reply is that, if everyone's values are equal, then no one may stop anyone for committing any crime. But this is a misunderstanding of moral equality and fairness: a man striking another, innocent, man down is putting his values and well-being above those of his victim, and there's nothing fair about that. As anarchist writer Benjamin Tucker wrote in my favorite quote about ethics, the only way to reestablish equality between the two is to prevent further victimization:

> When I describe a man as an invader, I cast no reflection upon him; I simply state a fact. Nor do I assert for a moment the moral inferiority of the invader's desire. I only declare the impossibility of simultaneously gratifying the invader's desire to invade and my desire to be let alone. That these desires are morally equal I cheerfully admit, but they cannot be equally realized. Since one must be subordinated to the other, I naturally prefer the subordination of the invader's, and am ready to co-operate with non-invasive persons to achieve that result.

You may ask why I put so much emphasis on this particular principle and not others. Of course I will discuss other ethical principles as we get to them, but the ends-in-themselves principle is a good summation of what makes an action ethical or unethical, because it is almost uniformly the case that unethical behavior involves treating people as a means to an end.

All other principles that people commonly consider to be ethical guidelines, such as being nice to others, the Golden Rule (and other principles based on reciprocity), human empathy and compassion, respecting other people's decisions, having consent from another person before acting on them, not harming or causing suffering to others, and so on, can be placed under the conceptual umbrella of "treating people as ends-in-themselves."

Likewise, it is rare to see suffering being inflicted without there being first objectification and dehumanization of the victim in some way: in all forms of prejudice, war, genocide, and so on, it is first necessary to implant the belief that the targeted group is somehow less human than us, in order to make mass violence against them acceptable. All women are heartless bitches and promiscuous gold-diggers, all black people are shiftless, criminals, and violent beasts, all Jews are social vermin and financial exploiters, and so on. They are objectified (i.e. defined as a narrow set of attributes instead of defined as human beings within their full individuality) and dehumanized (i.e. because of this negative, narrow definition, they are less than fully human).

People have different opinions about what "treating people as ends-in-themselves" concretely implies. There are obvious consequences (e.g. slavery is bad) and not-so-obvious consequences (e.g. is wage labor bad?). I believe that the presence of a hierarchy is sufficient reason to declare that a system treats people as means to an end.

A hierarchy is any social system where control is used in a way that is both *systemic* and *directed:*

1. The use of control must be *systemic*, that is to say, part of the system, not incidental to it. For instance, a man may mistreat his wife at an amusement park because he has been raised to believe that women are inferior. In that case, the hierarchy is not the amusement park, but sexism: the control was incidental to the amusement park as a system.

2. The use of control must be *directed*, that is to say, from one specific person or group of people- the superiors- to another specific person or group of people- the inferiors. In the case of sexism, the superiors are the men and the inferiors are the women and the gender non-conforming.

All hierarchies necessarily imply treating people as means to an end, because they are based on superiors ordering inferiors around in order to get them to bring about the objectives of the hierarchy. There are innumerable examples of hierarchies in our societies: governments, justice systems, militaries, corporations, jails, religions, cults, racism, genderism and sexism, nationalism, classism, to name only those. There is no area of our lives which is not strongly influenced by some hierarchy or hierarchies.

However, due to the topic of this book, one of these in particular interests us, and that's the family structure. It has the distinction of being by far the most intimate hierarchy: rarely do superiors and inferiors live, eat and sleep together to the extent that parents and children do. Parents can mold their children's beliefs and values in a way that doesn't really exist in other hierarchies: government try to mold their people's behavior but they can only do so through extensive and constant propaganda, cults try to brainwash people but the baseline personality always remains in the background, ready to reassert itself when the person is confronted with enough cognitive dissonance.

For these reasons, I think the family structure is by far the most rigorous hierarchy of all. This is also reflected in the abuse leveled at children by their parents. Because of the omerta surrounding child abuse (which I will discuss in chapter 4), it is extremely difficult to get accurate statistics. According to the United Nations (the UN Secretary-General's Study on Violence Against Children, 2006), 80% or more of children worldwide are victim of physical punishment, 223 million children were raped (more than 10% of all children at the time), and more than 100 million girls had circumcised genitals.

The situation in the Western world is not this bad, but not that good either. In the United States, a majority of parents approve of physical punishment, and a majority still use it. Rates of sexual abuse are reported as anywhere from 16% to 28%.

Whatever the exact numbers are, it is clear that violence and abuse by parents against their children is widespread and still generally accepted although it is now, for the most part, illegal. Laws have changed, but attitudes have not, and attitudes generally dictate how we see behavior.

The reason for this state of affairs is, I think, obvious for anyone who is willing to confront it: the family structure has the greatest inequality of power of any hierarchy. The superiors are grown adults, the inferiors are babies, little children, and teenagers, so there is generally a huge physical disparity. The omerta surrounding the family home ("a man's home is his castle") means that abuses will be vastly under-reported. There is general support for child abuse amongst the general population, as long as it's cloaked under the guise of "discipline."

All these factors lead to the conclusion that parents can, if they wish, abuse their children with little risk. Some parents do not want to abuse their children, obviously, and they are free to be magnanimous superiors, but their good behavior does not erase the existence of the hierarchy.

I know that parents who read this book (if there are any) will resist these facts, and I understand that. No one likes to have their privilege pointed out. But this book is about a new approach to procreative ethics based on childism and antinatalism: some level of hostility towards parents is inevitable and necessary.

For the sake of parrying the equally inevitable questions about my intentions, I will say that my childhood was about as good as any person has the right to expect. I have nothing against my parents and do believe that they did the best they could in raising me. I do think they could have done better, but that's true of anyone.

The positions I defend in this book are not the result of any sort of personal bitterness of vendetta against my parents, or any other parents. They are the result of years of reading, arguing, and introspection. That being said, I have nothing against people who have had bad parents and who wish to express their anger at that fact, either. That's not just what this book is about.

All of this was a rather roundabout way of getting to the point that the family structure is the most extreme form of hierarchy that exists, which means it is a perfect example of treating people as means to an end. Now, I have not discussed yet what form this treatment takes: this will be the subject of the next chapter.

Before I move on, I did want to address one ethical objection to this chapter. One reply that is often made when one discusses ethical principles is "what about the people who disagree with you?" What if some people disagree that we should treat people as ends-in-themselves?

But as I already pointed out, this principle is part and parcel of all the major principles of ethics that people believe in. To reject treating people as ends-in-themselves also means rejecting the principle of consent, the principle of reciprocity, empathy, and so on. Surely doing this is argumentative suicide.

Of course there are certain people who don't care about others at all; we call those people sociopaths. I grant that they, of all people, would reject the belief that they should treat people as ends-in-themselves, but I don't think anyone should be losing sleep over what sociopaths believe or do not believe.

I think a more serious source of disagreement would be people who accept the ends-in-themselves principle but do not think it applies to children. They would say something like this: "Of course we shouldn't treat other adults as means to an end, but we sometimes need to treat children as means to an end because..."

What follow this "because..." may vary, but it would most likely fall into one of the three categories of rationalizations for childism that I will analyze in chapter 4. Hopefully my discussions about childism in this book will demonstrate that there is no ethical or rational way to complete that sentence. Children should never be treated as means to an end.

Chapter 3
The Alignment Paradigm and the Domestication Hierarchy

The alignment paradigm

I've argued that children are treated as means to an end. But to what end?

It used to be that children served the purpose of cheap labor. Parents could exploit their children much more easily than they could exploit anyone else, so they put them to work on the family farm or the family business, and the father expected his sons to follow in his footsteps. This view has mostly fallen out of favor in Western societies.

Obviously parents' objectives in raising children vary wildly, so any answer will necessarily be a generality. But once we accept this, one answer in particular stands out: the child must be made to "fit in" with the rest of society. The child must hold the correct beliefs, act in a proper manner, feel what a normal person would feel, all in accordance with the social constructs of nationality, culture, gender, religion, intelligence, race, and so on. This is what I call the *alignment paradigm*.

A question naturally arises: how do parents determine what the correct beliefs are, what the proper manner of acting is, what feelings are normal in what situation? The answer is that the goal of the alignment is for the child to be successful, usually materially successful or relationally successful (or whatever else is the highest good in their society).

The connection is obvious in a very general sort of way: a person who follows the mores and expectations of their society will be more likely to be judged as worthy of success by that society. There are very few counter-culture elected politicians, CEOs, military officers. People who have opinions which are outside of the margins of discourse are not likely to be seen as credible by the general population, unless they gained that credibility in some other way (such as by becoming an entertainment celebrity).

The alignment paradigm means, in short, that the values of the child must be trampled in favor of those values that its parents consider conducive to "success." The needs, desires or feelings of the child must be suppressed at all costs, covertly if at all possible, coercively otherwise. This use of coercion is "normal" and "necessary," and therefore does not arouse suspicion.

From our very first day of existence on this planet, we are treated as if we have a gender, a race, a class, a religion, a nationality, a sexual orientation, and so on, even though all of these things are social constructs and therefore only apply to social agents (individuals who have a relative place in society based on their social interactions). A baby is not a social agent and therefore cannot have any of those things: a baby cannot, and does not, have a gender, a race, a class, a religion, a nationality, or a sexual orientation. There is no such thing as a "baby girl," a "black baby," a "middle class baby," a "Christian baby," an "American baby" or a "heterosexual baby."

I imagine that for many people this last statement will be seen as bizarre or even absurd. After all, designating babies as boys or girls is a matter of routine. The same is true for race, nationality and religion, but let's take gender as an example.

The popular myth is that gender is a biological fact, but there's no scientific evidence whatsoever of gender being biological[5]. Keep in mind that gender is not a description of XX or XY chromosomes, internal or external genitals, or hormone levels: that's sex, which is a biological fact. Gender, amongst other things, is the association of a group based on sex (male=man, female=woman) with stereotypes (e.g. "women are bad at math," "men aren't in touch with their feelings," "women are meant to be nurturing," "men are meant to be competitive and aggressive").

Gender is a social construct (meaning that it exists because it's widely accepted, not because it's based on reality), and as such it exists only as a relation: we signal our gender to others in the ways we dress, move, talk, and form relationships. Babies do none of these things because, again, they are not social agents, therefore they cannot have a gender. It makes no more sense to say that a baby has a gender than to say that a baby has a job or a credit record.

This is why, in case you're wondering, I use "it" when talking about children. This is not out of a desire to dehumanize children, but rather to make clear the fact that "he" and "she" are highly inappropriate, especially when talking about babies or young children. Unfortunately the English language has no good gender-neutral pronouns, so I have decided to use "it."

Gender is clearly a social construct that exists in order to support procreation. No matter the culture, women are always portrayed as passive, as caring, as dependent, and they are encouraged to procreate as a fulfillment of their womanhood. Men are portrayed as active, as competitive, as independent, and so they are encouraged to display their manhood by having a big family. Girls are encouraged to play with dolls and are raised to fantasize about the pageantry of weddings. Boys are told by the culture that they must have sex, and that they should see women and children as rewards.

Furthermore, consider that homophobia, in the West, is a big part of masculinity. Men will do a lot to distance themselves from being portrayed as homosexuals, and having children is a big marker of heterosexual virility. It proves, at least superficially, that you have had sex with women over and over, and that you are not a "faggot." The tension between repressed homosexuality and rejecting homosexuality is at the core of Western culture[6].

Much of the attraction of these social constructs, and one of the main reasons why parents want to reproduce them through the socialization of their children, lies in the general belief that they are natural, i.e. that they are rooted in biology. But the main reason is because they believe that the child must accept them in order to be "normal," and ultimately, "successful."

Children who refuse to conform to the socialization they're given must be set back on the right path. In the case of gender, that means either forcing the child to play with the "right" toys, wear the "right" clothes and have the "right" hobbies, regardless of what they want, or submit the child to untested puberty blockers and major surgery which will affect them for the rest of their lives (not to mention the brutal genital mutilation committed against intersex babies at birth). Either way, gender non-conforming children are seen as an aberration which must be set right.

Socialization is the most important factor in determining the kind of person we become. We were all subjected to it and none of us were immune to its effects. We were all "normalized," to the extent that our parents, our schools and the media were willing to "normalize" us. And, as I said before, the goal of that normalization was for us to be "successful."

Starting from this point, we can begin by asking: why would becoming "successful" be the objective of a child's development? The fact that children develop is a biological fact, not a human creation, and therefore is inherently value-neutral. Where does the value of "success" come in?

The honest answer to that question would probably be that parents wants "their" children to be successful because it makes them look good and confirms that they are "good parents." The success of the children creates the success of the parents. But the ego of the parents is not a rational justification of the way a child should be raised.

The answer you're most likely to get is that the parents want "their" children to be happy. The implicit premise is that successful people are happy. Yet there is no scientific evidence of that: quite the contrary, there is evidence that neither success, ambition or money lead people to happiness.

I've already quoted David Benatar on optimistic biases. There's another mechanism at work, which is called hedonic adaptation. This refers to the fact that happiness levels remain relatively stable throughout our lives, and that extreme levels of happiness (either low or high) do not last. Like a rubber band, our happiness level eventually bounces back from any change, even winning the lottery or becoming a paraplegic. As explained by Shane Frederick and George Loewenstein in Well-Being: The Foundations of Hedonic Psychology:

> Although hedonic adaptation confers enormous benefits by reducing the subjective effects of adverse conditions, it

44

has associated costs as well. The most obvious cost of hedonic adaption is that it occurs for goods as well as bads, creating what Brickman and Campbell (1971) have called the "hedonic treadmill" — the tendency for transitory satisfactions to eventually give way to indifference or even dissatisfaction.

Now, I'm no psychologist, but it seems to me that if happiness is a stable datum, then there's little point in trying to create happier adults by making them "successful." Of course there's nothing wrong with wanting people to be happy, and we know the kinds of things that make people temporarily happy, but it is not really clear at all what makes people happy people in the long term.

It may be argued that parents have their children's best interests in mind, and that we should therefore pardon their incompetence. But there is a further problem here, which I've already alluded to: the alignment paradigm is profoundly childist, i.e. prejudiced against children, because it assumes that a child's freedom of speech, thought and action are irrelevant compared to its future, that the child is a means to an end, said end being its future self. Their present self is being sacrificed for their future self. Keep in mind the famous expression "children are our future"... not *their* present, but *our* future.

We certainly would not admit of an adult's freedoms being curtailed because we expect it to make them better people in the future. People would rightly point out the paternalistic (pater=father) nature of such interventions, and complain that this means "treating them like children." But why should we treat *children* this way?

Take the case of religion. Parents may force a child to attend a church it does not want to attend. It may not want to attend any church at all. We think it normal for parents to impose religion on their children. In all cases, this is done without the consent of the child, as we believe children's consent is irrelevant. Even atheist parents, who usually support freedom of religion as well as freedom from religion, will readily defend the right of religious parents to indoctrinate their children.

Because of childism, we do not see children as human beings, otherwise the equation would be obvious:

1. Human beings have freedom of religion.
2. Children are human beings.
3. Therefore children have freedom of religion.

This is an equation I will come back to again and again, because it is the fundamental truth of the situation. Just as we often refuse to see women as full human beings, or people of races we don't like as full human beings, or poor people as full human beings, we refuse to see children as full human beings. I will get into the rationalizations used to support this in the next chapter.

If there's one thing I've learned from discussing

childism, it's that parents will typically become enraged if you question their authority. This is no more surprising than the rage expressed by any individual who is part of a privileged group when confronted about their privilege. Parents, having near-complete control over another human being, have a great deal of privilege as parents. The source of this privilege is the ability to convince themselves, and the rest of society, that their child is not a full human being.

Given the overwhelming public support for freedom of religion (implicitly, for adults only), the fact that we refuse to grant it for children demonstrates the power of childism in molding opinions. If there is no possible reason why we should take away freedom of religion to an adult, then there are no possible reasons why we should take away freedom of religion to a child.

A further problem with granting the right to adults but not to children is that such uneven application is profoundly contradictory. If children do not have freedom of religion, then adults don't either.

This can be demonstrated by two hypothetical situations. Person A was indoctrinated in Christianity at a very young age and remains a Christian as an adult because they are completely invested in the all-encompassing and self-validating beliefs they were taught. Person B was indoctrinated in Christianity in childhood, rebelled against it, and later on changes denominations, or becomes an atheist, or simply drops out of the whole religion debate.

Person A has been trapped in some self-validating belief (such as the infallibility of the Bible) and is not free to think outside of it. Person B changed their allegiances as a reaction the indoctrination they received, not as a form of freedom. Neither of them had freedom of religion at any point. And yet we believe that at 18 years of age A and B gained freedom of religion, when they already got indoctrinated in a religion from the youngest age and that this indoctrination was were constantly reinforced by their parents, school and society for more than ten years.

It simply doesn't make any sense. It would be like breaking a baby's legs, never teaching it to stand up, keeping it sitting or lying down, and then, at 18 years old, claiming that it now has the freedom to walk. Who would call that freedom?

This principle applies to all socialization, not just religious socialization. It makes no sense to claim that adults are free to be who they are, and are responsible for being who they are, if they've been molded by 18 years of constant socialization, if their opportunities were molded by the kind of family they were born in, if the scope of their world was limited to what their parents exposed them to.

Social constructs have no independent existence, and therefore depend on socialization to continue to exist. The alignment paradigm describes why and how our society reproduces itself, the source of the continuity in the way people see themselves and the world from generation to generation. It also sets the tone for the future adults by telling them that conformity ensures happiness, and that if they are not happy, it must be because they fail to conform to social standards (including the life blueprint).

Now, I've stated that the alignment paradigm is a general statement. Not all parents follow this paradigm: there are parents who are very well aware of socialization and who try to minimize its effects on their children. But such parents are headed for failure, for two main reasons:

1. Even the most intelligent and conscious parents are unaware of how much they reveal to their children through their behavior. Little children are discovery machines, and they pick up easily on latent racist or sexist attitudes from their parents.

2. Parents are only one side of the socialization process: a child's friends and other parents, the media it's exposed to, the school system, are all part of that process.

On that second point, let me quote Cordelia Fine, from Delusions of Gender:

> '[A] parent,' suggests [psychologist Barbara David], 'no matter how loving or loved, cannot be a model for appropriate gender behaviour, unless the child's exposure to the wider world (for example, through friendship groups and the media) suggests

that the parent is a representative or prototypical male or female'.

If so, the egalitarian parent can look forward to being undermined on a daily basis. For, as it happens, neither children, nor children's media, are renowned for their open-minded approach to gender roles.

Through the alignment paradigm, parents are a great help to the formation of prejudice, but they are by no means the only influence.

The domestication hierarchy

The second concept I wanted to discuss in this chapter stems from the following question: if we posit that the family structure is a hierarchy where the parents are the superiors and the children are the inferiors, then what is the justification for this hierarchy?

For example, we say that the hierarchy between workers and bosses is justified by property rights, we say that the hierarchy of races is justified by innate biological limits on intelligence and temperament, we say that the hierarchy between men and women is justified by innate biological differences in abilities and temperament, and so on. What is the hierarchy between parents and children based on?

We must add to this a further, crucial point: the

stereotype of the child, of childishness, cuts through prejudice barriers. In The Culture of Conformity, Patrick Hogan delineates two metaphorical frameworks, which he calls domains, used to discuss race: the domain of maturity and the domain of animalcy. The former is divided in four categories: children, adolescents, adults and elders.

> Adulthood is, of course, the standard by which the others are measured, and it is the model for the dominant group...
>
> The infantile model yields a conception of a status group that is asexual or presexual, naive, intellectually limited to basic studies, lacking an internalized morality yet fundamentally good-natured and thus inclined to follow parental guidance, playful and friendly, chattering, and cute. The adolescent model, in contrast, is highly and compulsively sexual, clever and cunning, still intellectually limited (though somewhat less so), actively rebellious against parental authority and morality, aggressive and unfriendly, inscrutably silent, and either ugly or powerfully sexually attractive.
>
> It is not difficult to see that the former is one of the most persistent models for women in our culture... This is [also] the view of Africans as happy, banjo-playing folk, apt to a grade school education only... friendly and loquacious.

This tells us that this hierarchy is not just about parenting or the family structure, but about something deeper which has to do with how we view children, which is then used as the (partial) basis for other stereotypes.

I believe that central to the way we view children, especially babies and young children, is the concept of wildness: they are "wild," "immature," devoid of any morality, master manipulators, born evil (according to Christian writ), and they must be "domesticated" through imitating adults and absorbing their commands. This mindset has been ingrained in the way we raise babies all the way to the modern era (Dr. Spock advocating being firm against babies' manipulations by not responding to their crying, for example, a concept which is still being popularized today despite its profound childism and idiocy).

Perhaps the most famous expression of the "wildness" and innate amorality/evil of children is the novel Lord of the Flies. For those of you who haven't read it, Lord of the Flies is the story of a group of boys shipwrecked on a deserted island. The children progressively descend "back" into "wildness" (which is represented as Satan, the Lord of the Flies), to the point where they start killing each other and set fire to the island's forest before they are rescued.

Even though Lord of the Flies has recently breathed new life into it, this worldview is not new, by a long shot. Here is a quote from Elisabeth Young-Bruehl describing Aristotle's philosophy in her book Childism (a book which I will quote more extensively later):

> Aristotle's assumptions about children- that they are possessions and lack reasoning ability- are childist... The idea that children are by nature meant to be owned by their male parent and that they lack reason has justified treating them like slaves and like immature, unformed persons without the active qualities, the developmental thrust, the proto-reasoning and choosing, and the individuality that contemporary developmentalists now recognize in them...
>
> The need that limits Aristotle's worldview is a desire for control and domination. Children are born wild and undomesticated and must be controlled, and women, as unreasoning beings, are not able to do this controlling.

She goes on to discuss the connection between ancient views about conception, where the male is the only active agent and the woman only a receptacle for sperm, with sexism and childism. In general, we can say that where children are devalued, women are usually devalued as well, especially since in such societies women are usually seen as little more than passive agents of procreation.

The alignment paradigm I've previously discussed

has been derived from the more modern view that children start as "blank slates" which must merely be educated and domesticated. The dominant view in the past was that children were evil and selfish, and therefore needed to be beaten, tricked, or otherwise violently reined in.

In either case, childhood stands in for humans in the state of nature: people (like Christians) who believe that humanity is innately sinful and evil will necessarily believe that children are sinful and evil, and people who believe that the state of nature is "wild" but well-intentioned and capable of reform (as our ancestors viewed "savages") will necessary believe that children are "wild" but well-intentioned. These lead to different forms of childism, the former more violent and centered around "discipline," and the latter more paternalistic and centered around "education." And those few crackpots who believe that human beings are innately good (or mostly good) but corrupted by society will tend to adopt anti-childist views similar to the ones I discuss in this book (which I freely admit are also crackpot views).

The dual stereotypes described by Hogan show the positive and negative interpretations of wildness. Being devoid of morality is seen as a need for guidance and naivete, as well as rebellion and aggression. Being immature and wild is seen as playfulness and chattiness (attributes which are seen as useless and not serious, but cute), as well as unfriendliness, sexuality and rebellion.

I realize that what I am calling wildness has nothing to do with actual wildness, and the process of domesticating a child has little in common with the domestication of animals. I am using the terms as metaphors for the way people see children. Childists certainly seem to think children are wild animals that need to be domesticated. Here is an example, perhaps from the extreme end of the scale, of this view, from Biblical Insights in Child Training by Red Bradley (yes, "training" is in the title, and this is from a DVD course made in this millennium):

> Every baby starts life as a little savage. He is completely selfish and self-centered: he wants what he wants—his bottle, his mother's attention, his playmate's toys, his uncle's watch, or whatever. Deny him these and he seethes with rage and aggressiveness which would be murderous were he not so helpless. He is dirty; he has no morals, no knowledge and no developed skills. This means that all children, not just certain children, but all children are born delinquent. If permitted to continue in their self-centered world of infancy, given free reign to their impulsive actions to satisfy each want—every child would grow up a criminal, a killer, a thief, and a rapist.

This finds its source in the Christian belief that we are born evil, and that therefore a baby is evil, as bizarre as that may seem. The view that we are innately evil has a lot of proponents, and not just religious people. The difference between them lies in what they believe keeps society from complete criminal chaos: some believe it is good Christian child indoctrination, some believe it is the fear of God, some believe it is the State and its laws, some believe it is the "thin veil of civilization," and others believe we already are in a state of complete criminal chaos[7].

The view that we are born evil is popular with hucksters of all kinds, because they know that in order to sell you a solution they must first sell you a problem. In order to sell you salvation, they must first sell you damnation, otherwise what's the point? I believe that the whole "babies are evil" thing is only a by-product of this process, but it has quite permeated our public discourse about children.

Like gender and race, domestication is not just a basis for prejudice but also a model against which all children are measured. A "good child" is one which follows the infantile model and a "bad child" is one which follows the adolescent model.

But whether they are "good" or "bad," all children are by definition undeveloped persons: only adults are fully developed persons. This means that children do not have full human rights and cannot have full human rights, as only fully developed persons "deserve" human rights and the human rights of children must be suppressed in order to further their development.

The objective of pedagogy is to use children's lives as means to an end, this end being the future person

56

they will become once they are developed. Whatever method is used to develop a child's character, demanding and strict or relaxed and permissive, the desired end goal (desired by the parents, not by the child) is always a well-adapted, productive person (well-adapted and productive according to social standards), and the justification is the need to "domesticate" the child.

I've already discussed socialization, which is a big part of this domestication process. But of course domestication involves more than that. For one thing, some children rebel against their socialization, probably due to their personality clashing too much with their assigned social roles. So there is a need for punishment, or as it's euphemistically called, "discipline" (actual discipline is a personality trait and has nothing to do with punishment or incentives), to keep children on the "right path."

Punishment can take many forms, including physical abuse, verbal abuse, emotional abuse, and neglect. Now, I am not saying that parents always punish children grievously. Sometimes emotional abuse can be something light, such as taking away a favorite toy or activity, and physical abuse can be something as light as a slap on the hand. But in all cases, they are things that we would never tolerate one adult doing to another adult; in the case of physical abuse, they are things which are not even legal to do to another adult, at least not without consent.

57

The basic principle at play here is simple: *if children are human beings, and we should not do these things to human beings, then we should not do these things to children.*

I imagine parents reading this will be outraged and argue that I am oversimplifying. Obviously we need to punish children, otherwise they'll be "spoiled" (i.e. useless for the parents or for society, like spoiled food is useless for consumption). Obviously we need to punish children, otherwise they'll get "out of hand" (i.e. become uncontrollable by the parents or by society). Obviously some form of punishment is necessary. Some people punish too harshly, and we should blame them, but you shouldn't blame me. I only want what's best for my children.

But this misses the point. My disagreement does not lie at the level of how hard to punish children. My disagreement lies with the purpose of pedagogy itself: I believe that the very notion of "domesticating" children so they are properly "aligned" with society is an artificial goal which serves the sole purpose of reproducing institutions, not for the good of the child (or, for that matter, the good of the parents, although I couldn't care less about that).

My position is that we should act only for the good of the child, and that we should be on the side of the child. Any other position is inherently childist. As I will explain later, all pedagogies are basically ways to assert control over children.

As such, my position is not that some parents are "doing it wrong," but that insofar as all parenting is nothing more than a power struggle which goes against the child's natural development, there is no way to "do it right." And if a parent stops engaging in that power struggle and begins to engage with the child on an equal footing, he or she then stops being a parent (and this would be opposed by other parents as the sin of permissiveness, which can only "spoil" a child).

Now back to the argument. It seems very simple, but it needs to be spelled out: *punishing children as "discipline" is bad because children are human beings.* I say it needs to be spelled out because you will routinely read people who are against corporal punishment make an argument on the basis of consequences: that it predisposes children to become violent later in life, that it is correlated with alcoholism and depression later in life, that it is correlated with hyperactivity and emotional problems, that it lowers IQ, and so on.

Whether these arguments are true or not (and I have no particular reason to doubt them), they are completely irrelevant to the issue at hand. For one thing, they imply that if corporal punishment did not have these deleterious effects, then it would be all right to use it. But surely this can't be right: if corporal punishment is wrong, then it is wrong regardless of its consequences. We don't simply stop prosecuting crimes when they have no visible consequences.

We would never say, for example, that drunk driving is wrong because letting people drive drunk will lower their motor skills or that kidnapping is wrong because the victim will be more likely to have low self-esteem in the future. These considerations are not relevant. Drunk driving is wrong because it puts other people at risk of harm, kidnapping is wrong because it is a harm, and people have the right to be protected from harm.

Now granted, there are people who think measuring consequences is a valid ethical position. But even from a consequentialist perspective, the reasoning doesn't make much sense. Surely any given act of corporal punishment does not have a big consequence on any child's alcoholism or depression in the long-term, but any given act of corporal punishment does have one big, inescapable consequence: a child has been hurt.

But the bigger problem is that this sort of argument reduces children as means to an end, and again the end is proper alignment with society. People think these arguments make sense because being violent, alcoholic, depressed, or hyperactive are not aligned with our conception of the ideal person, or even of a normal person. They also don't help make a "successful" adult, especially lower IQ. But there's no particular reason for us to believe that the end of a child is an aligned adult or a "successful" adult. Children are human beings and should be treated as individuals, not as means to some arbitrary end.

And the proof that childism is really ingrained in our thinking is that even the most fairness-minded people, who don't have an ounce of child-hatred in their minds, will still talk like this as if it was a perfectly normal thing to say. Like racism and sexism, prejudice is hard to see unless you know what to look for.

We cringe when we hear what people in the past were saying about races and sexes, even though they no doubt thought of themselves as fair-minded as well. There's no reason to believe that the same process won't happen fifty years or a century from now with the childism that permeates our discourse. People will one day look with revulsion to the concept that parents should spank their children.

Now, most of us still happen to believe that spanking is a good thing, or at least a necessary thing. Well, I hope I am not teaching anything to anyone here, but spanking is a sexual act, and therefore inflicting it on children is sexual assault (if you don't believe me, then go to any site that hosts porn videos and search for "spanking"). The buttocks are an erogenous zone because they have many nerves which are connected to the sexual nerve system, like our genitals. That's why spanking can give people sexual pleasure.

These are facts that people would rather not discuss, but they are not exactly obscure facts. And you can gloss over them all you want. For example, you can argue that spanking over clothes is not sexual assault, but the same nerve endings are affected in either case. You might as well argue that fondling a woman's breasts over her clothes shouldn't be called sexual assault, because after all her breasts were covered up. I'm pretty sure a female victim of such an action would disagree with that glib assessment.

Another common form of "discipline" is emotional blackmail, e.g. "you do something wrong and I will revoke some of your privileges." It may seem strange to call this blackmail, but what is the relation between, for example, a child not getting out of bed and being forbidden to watch television? The "or you won't get to watch television" is clearly a threat designed to cow the child, not to help the child want to get up but to force the child to get up. Apart from that context, it simply doesn't make any sense.

Well, that is an emotionally abusive action. The parent is using the child's attachment to something (e.g. watching television) to force it to do something unrelated. Although obviously no money changes hands, that is strongly analogous to blackmail, and the goal is to enforce obedience through fear. In a commentary for CNN.com published on September 18, 2014, commentator Ruben Navarrette is refreshingly direct and honest about the purpose of spanking:

> Fear is essential to respect. Children won't do what we tell them to do, unless -- at some level -- they fear the consequences that will come from not doing it.

Another process, which is far, far more insidious, much worse, and much more evil than any punishment, is the internalization of the punishment. This happens when the child comes to honestly believe that it deserved the punishment it got, and that it must actively participate in its own domestication.

This is a horrific process. But equally horrific is the fact that many people who are against corporal punishment, who are against child abuse, explicitly argue that this is the desired end result of pedagogy! Here is an example, from professor of philosophy Gary Bartlett (italics mine):

> Corporal punishment has been found to be associated with *lower internalization of moral norms.* Spanking, along with other disciplinary methods involving overt external pressure, may teach a child to avoid misbehavior in order to avoid being spanked, rather than teaching him why that behavior in itself is bad – so that he will learn to avoid the behavior only when the parent is present. So compared to less overtly punitive methods, spanking may be less effective at reducing recurrence of misbehavior, because *it does less to instill an internal motivation to avoid such behavior.*

I find this quote to be a chilling display of the hatred which people like Bartlett feel towards children. According to him, the problem with spanking is not that it aims to generate obedience, but that the obedience it generates is not internalized enough! Children must not only be made to obey parental control, but they must internalize it so well that it becomes part of their personal identity.

Comparisons with 1984, mind-bending cults, and other totalitarian mind control systems come to mind. If the objective of punishment is not just to stop disobedience, but to make the child sincerely want to obey, then any possibility of a child having freedom of thought, or any freedom at all, is gone out the window.

If he wrote the same thing about people in a cult or a dictatorship, such as "cults should not use corporal punishment because it does less to instill an internal motivation to obey the leader," he would no doubt have been horrified and would have never published it. Again, it is only because childism is the default that people like Bartlett, who are opposed to corporal punishment but have not examined their beliefs about children, can write such amazing statements without even realizing what they're writing.

It remains implicit in Bartlett's reasoning that the parent sets the standard for "misbehavior," and that therefore the parent is justified in trying to enforce that standard on the child. Only the parent's moral norms matter. The child's moral norms (which, according to childist logic, do not exist anyway) do not matter in any way, shape or form. There is no place for disagreement or compromise. Transpose this discourse to the world of adults and you get a Pol Pot or a Jim Jones.

No wonder people see nothing wrong in forcing children into existence. That seems like peccadillos compared to the even worse ways in which people think about children.

The demand for internalization is based on the premise that the parent's values are necessarily (by virtue of being those of the parent) superior to those of the child, and that a parent's ability to give orders also grants the right or freedom to enforce values. Both of these premises are wildly wrong.

For one, there is no reason at all to believe that a parent's values are **necessarily** superior: it may be that some parents are right about one thing that their children are not right about, but that does not make them right about everything. More to the point, we could tell when they are right only by examining the claims made by the parent and those made by the child: a parent is not right simply by virtue of being a parent. Becoming a parent does not grant one some kind of magical ability to always be right. Sometimes a parent is right and their child is wrong, but also vice-versa. To believe otherwise is fantasy.

As for the second premise, I will analyze it further in the next chapter under the heading of *the order/value gap*. Basically, there is no way to logically start from an order (e.g. given by a parent) and conclude that the recipient of the order must change their values solely on the basis of that order (or any number of orders). The child does change its values, not because it has been persuaded (orders are not a form of persuasion), but because it has been indoctrinated or cowed.

There is even more dangerous poison contained within this toxic concept of internalization, and here is a poison that does a great deal of damage to people: because children are raised to believe that parents "discipline" them because they love them, children come to, subconsciously or consciously, equate love with abuse. The child who grows us with sexual assaults or physical punishment accepts those things as standards of love or caring, and may even seek them out as signals of love or caring. People trapped in abusive relationships, by and large, do not see what's being done to them as abuse (and when they do, it's too dangerous for them to leave) because they were raised to believe that abuse is love.

None do evil more cheerfully and with more conviction than those who believe they are doing it in the name of helping others. I do not dispute that most parents have good intentions, but that only makes them more dangerous. All children have to become independent from their parents at some point, not just physically but also mentally, and it is much harder to detach oneself from abuse disguised as love than it is to detach oneself from abuse that is consciously understood as abuse.

With the alignment paradigm and the domestication

hierarchy, I've given a general idea of the chain of childism that occurs once a child is born. While giving birth to a child is a childist act, it is not by far the only one.

But why talk about these other steps at all? As I've discussed earlier, natalism implies that children are nothing more than abstract objects, numbers, that we can stack up to solve social problems or accumulate happiness. A necessary condition of natalism is hiding the third side of the equation, which is the child; natalism and awareness of childism cannot logically coexist.

The alignment paradigm, the domestication hierarchy, "discipline," and internalization, are demonstrations that children are seen by their parents and by society as means to an end. Now that the roadmap has been set up, I will examine childism itself more closely in the next chapter.

Chapter 4
Childism

Being on the side of the child

Two individuals in particular have had a profound influence on pointing out the popular misconceptions and prejudices we have about childhood. Since my position against childism, and that of many others, finds its conceptual roots in these two individuals, I thought I should talk about their work here and highlight why they are so important. These two people are Alice Miller, German psychologist who is most well-known for her works on the consequences of child abuse, and A.S. Neill, British educator and founder of Summerhill School.

Alice Miller was a trained psychotherapist who wrote a wide range of books (twelve of which have been translated to English) about the impact of child abuse on development and character. A reader of her books may see her point of view change from a somewhat skeptical Freudian approach to a rejection of the Freudian approach, which she eventually identified as being fundamentally against the examination of childhood trauma.

But in all her books there is one basic principle that comes up again and again: the most important thing any adult can do is *to be on the side of the child*. A child must have at least one adult in their life who is on their side and that they can confide in; if this condition is present, then the child will be able to analyze and deal with the trauma they go through, otherwise they will not be able to do so.

As she summarizes in her article The Essential Role of an Enlightened Witness in Society:

> Anyone addressing the problem of child abuse is likely to be faced with a very strange finding: it has frequently been observed that parents who abuse their children tend to mistreat and neglect them in ways resembling their own treatment as children, without any conscious memory of their own experiences. It is well known that fathers who bully their children through sexual abuse are usually unaware that they had themselves suffered the same abuse. It is mostly in therapy, even if ordered by the courts, that they discover, stupefied, their own history, and realize thereby that for years they have attempted to act out their own scenario, just to get rid of it.
>
> How can this be explained? After studying the matter for years, it seems clear to me that information about abuse inflicted during childhood is recorded in our body cells as a sort of memory, linked to repressed anxiety. If, lacking the aid of an enlightened witness, these memories fail to break through to consciousness, they often compel the person to violent acts that reproduce the abuse

suffered in childhood, which was repressed in order to survive.

As this quote also indicates, she highlights the fact that any given act of child abuse is not an isolated act that should be analyzed in isolation, but rather part of a cycle of abuse. Children who were the victims of unresolved abuse become parents who inflict abuse on their own children, generally as revenge against their past abusers. But since they cannot inflict abuse on their parents, they do it on the people that are most vulnerable and under their control, their children. This she calls the repetition compulsion.

Through her psychology work, she also highlights the ways in which people with unresolved abuse issues make excuses for their abusive parents. Because we were all raised to respect our parents and to believe that any victimization we feel towards our parents is our own fault, it's very difficult to confront the reality of abuse. Unless a child was a victim of brutal beatings or severe sexual assault, people simply will not take the child's side. People are routinely gaslighted by their parents, by therapists, and by society about the reality of child abuse.

Alice Miller is a strong figure in childism awareness for many reasons. For one, she had the courage, as a psychotherapist whose job depended on accepting the *status quo*, to publicly reject the tenets of Freudian analysis and expose how such tenets really serve to hide the reality of child abuse, by rejecting the child's experience and labeling it "Oedipus complex" or "sexual drives" (i.e. it's always really the child's fault). From her book Banished Knowledge:

> It is only from adults that an unloved child learns to hate or torment and to disguise... feelings with lies and hypocrisy. That is why, when the child has grown up, he or she will say that children require norms and disciplining: this lie provides access to adult society, a lie that permeates all pedagogy and, to this day, psychoanalysis. The young child knows no lies, is prepared to take at their face value such words as truth, love, and mercy as heard in religious instruction in school. Only on finding out that his naivete is cause for ridicule does the child learn to dissemble. The child's upbringing teaches him the patterns of the destructive behavior that will later be interpreted by experts as the result of an innate destructive drive. Anyone daring to question this assertion will be smiled at for being naive, as if that person had never come in contact with children and didn't know "how they can get on your nerves." For at least since the days of Sigmund Freud, it has been known in "progressive" circles that children come into this world with a death drive and might kill us all if we didn't ward off "the first indications."

Alice Miller is also important because she discussed

the fact that fundamentally all pedagogy, not just the really bad ones, goes counter to the development of the child. From her book For Your Own Good:

> In contrast to generally accepted beliefs and to the horror of pedagogues, I cannot attribute any positive significance to the word pedagogy. I see it as self-defense on the part of adults, a manipulation deriving from their own lack of freedom and their insecurity, which I can certainly understand: although I cannot overlook the inherent dangers... There is in the word pedagogy the suggestion of certain goals that the charge is meant to achieve--and this limits his or her possibilities for development from the start...
>
> My antipedagogic position is not directed against a specific type of pedagogical ideology but against all pedagogical ideology per se, even if it is of an anti-authoritarian nature.
>
> I am convinced of the harmful effects of training for the following reason: all advice that pertains to raising children betrays more or less clearly the numerous, variously clothed needs of the adult. Fulfillment of these needs not only discourages the child's development but actually prevents it. This also hold true when the adult is honestly convinced of acting in the child's best interests.

This is particularly important because it addresses the common belief that there is a fundamental difference between "bad pedagogy" and "good pedagogy," as well as the "bad apples" excuse. Miller is clear that there is no easy out for advocates of parenting, no excuse they can fall back upon to separate those parents that go "too far" from those who don't.

Finally, Alice Miller's message is profoundly anti-childist because her take-away message, the summary of her attempts to persuade parents and society, can be summarized in the following:

Children need adults who are on their side. Always be on the side of the child.

This is an eye-opener for many of her readers, because it is a message which is singularly unusual (and that demonstrates how childist our societies are). People pay lip service to children, mainly to use them as rhetorical devices ("think of the children!") or as a focus of moral outrage ("children are taking drugs/having sex/getting stupider than the children of this other race!"), but rarely do we hear anyone actually taking a child's side unless the child was victimized in such a bad way that one simply cannot do otherwise (e.g. repeated child rape, brutal physical treatment, death). Even then, there are still people ready to rationalize a child's death (anti-vaccination advocates defending children dying of easily preventable diseases, fundamentalist Christians defending potentially lethal punishment methods, and so on).

A. S. Neill founded Summerhill School in 1921 (he died in 1973, but the work is continued by his daughter). He was inspired in doing so by the works of Homer Lane with what we call "juvenile delinquants." Homer Lane pioneered the concept of child self-regulation, where the rules are proposed and voted on by the children themselves, and more generally the importance of freedom and autonomy in children's lives: in short, the need to treat them like human beings. Neill took these principles and adapted them to a school setting, creating the first democratic school (and still one of the most influential).

> [W]e set out to make a school in which we should allow children freedom to be themselves. In order to do this, we had to renounce all discipline, all direction, all suggestion, all moral training, all religious instruction...
>
> What is Summerhill like? Well, for one thing, lessons are optional. Children can go to them or stay away from them- for years if they want to. There is a timetable- but only for the teachers.[8]

Students may attend as many classes, or as few classes, as they wish. Their education is entirely dependent on how much, and what, they are willing to learn, in short their natural interests.

Rules and regulations regarding children's lives are entirely set by a general vote, with every person (staff and students) getting one vote.

> Summerhill is a self-governing school, democratic in form. Everything connected with social, or group, life, including punishment for social offenses, is settled by vote at the Saturday night General Meeting.
>
> Each member of the teaching staff (including houseparents) and each child, regardless of his age, has one vote. My vote carries the same weight as that of a seven-year-old...
>
> Summerhill's self-government has no bureaucracy. There is a different chairman at each General Meeting, and the secretary's job is voluntary.

A.S. Neill founded Summerhill School not only on new educational principles but also on a worldview which was profoundly anti-childist. He rejected the notion that children are born amoral or evil and must be "domesticated." Rather the contrary, he believed that children can only develop fully if they are free to play and actually have a childhood, be children, instead of being imprisoned in schools.

> My view is that a child is innately wise and realistic. If left to himself without adult suggestion of any kind, he will develop as far as he is capable of developing...

The most frequent question asked by Summerhill visitors is, 'Won't the child turn round and blame the school for not making him learn arithmetic or music?' The answer is that young Freddy Beethoven and young Tommy Einstein will refuse to be kept away from their respective spheres.

The function of the child is to live his own life- not the life that his anxious parents think he should live, nor a life according to the purpose of the educator who thinks he knows what is best. All this interference and guidance on the part of adults only produces a generation of robots.

You cannot make children learn music or anything else without to some degree converting them into will-less adults...

One could, with some truth, claim that the evils of civilization are due to the fact that no child has ever had enough play. To put it differently, every child has been hothoused into being an adult long before he has reached adulthood.

More than any other principle, this is, perhaps, the core of anti-childism: the refusal to believe any wild ideas about children being innately incapable or evil. Of course children are often naturally selfish, as they should be and as we should let them be. There's nothing wrong about a developing individual being selfish, to the extent that it helps that development.

This, I think, is the central lesson we can get from Summerhill School. Every other principle of Summerhill School which differentiates it from other schools can be derived from it: the democratic functioning and self-regulation, the fact that students and staff all have one vote per person, the students' choices of classes, are all natural consequences of the belief that children are competent, at least in the areas that are of interest to them, and not innately amoral or evil. They can be made amoral or evil by their socialization or by abuse, but this is an evil coming from adults, not from the children.

> Self-regulation implies a belief in human nature, a belief that there is not, and never was, original sin. Self-regulation means the right of a baby to live freely without outside authority. It means the baby feeds when it is hungry; that it becomes clean in habits only when it wants to; that it is never stormed at nor spanked; that it shall always be loved and protected. Of course, self-regulation, like any theoretical idea, is dangerous if not combined with common sense.

Just as for Alice Miller, I would say that A.S. Neill is primarily preoccupied, not with choosing a "better" set of values that should be enforced on the child, but on being on the side of the child and its values. In fact, Neill himself said that his position in favor of personal freedoms for children meant being "on the side of the child" (according to Richard Bailey in his book A.S. Neill).

It is particularly interesting to me that both individuals (Miller and Neill) used this phrase "on the side of the child," especially since they meant something rather different by it. Miller used it in connection with having at least one adult in a child's life who was sympathetic to the child, who did not try to justify the parents' behavior and to blame the child. Neill was referring to the practice of children having the freedom and space to develop without parental harm or imposition. He reckoned that having children be away from their family most of the year was the best thing for children's independence, and that it was often the time when they went back to their families that was the most damaging.

But even though they meant something different by it, they both point to the same principle: *the refusal to marginalize, or argue against, children's feelings, desires and values*. This principle is necessary in order to realize the existence of childism, and the necessity of anti-childism. Miller and Neill were able to argue against child abuse, child indoctrination, and the interference in children's development, because they were first able to recognize the existence and nature of childism in their respective spheres (for Miller, psychotherapy and the rationalizations for corporal punishment; for Neill, schooling and the rationalizations for the forced schooling of children).

What is childism?

As the concept of childism studies is very much new, there is as of yet no consensus on definitions. In her book Childism, Elisabeth Young-Bruehl defines it as such:

> Drawing on a comparative study of prejudice forms, then, childism can be defined thus: a prejudice against children on the ground of a belief that they are property and can (or even should) be controlled, enslaved, or removed to serve adult needs.

Historically, the first known reference to childism as prejudice against children comes from a 1975 paper called Childism that was published in the journal Psychiatric Annals[9]. In it, psychiatrists Chester M. Pierce and Gail B. Allen define childism as such:

> Childism is the automatic presumption of superiority of any adult over any child; it results in the adult's needs, desires, hopes, and fears taking unquestioned precedence over those of the child.

Although these two definitions show a difference in approaches, they have some important commonalities: first, they establish a hierarchy between adults and children, second, they posit that adults are the superiors and that they seek to control children, and third, they point out the irrational nature of this control.

The latter is illustrated in Young-Bruehl's definition through the belief that children are property (which is irrational because human beings are not, and should not, be property) and that children should serve adult needs (which is irrational because it is children who have needs that must be met by adults, and adults' needs have little to no relevance to the child's development), and in Pierce and Allen's definition through the superiority of adults taking "unquestioned" precedence (anything unquestioned is necessarily irrational, as no premise can be rational unless it is open to doubt and questioning).

Furthermore, I agree with Young-Bruehl that we can profitably draw from other forms of prejudice in order to understand childism. Sexism, racism, anti-semitism, ableism, classism, and so on, are far more similar than they are different, and the frameworks we use to understand those can also be applied to childism.

For instance, all forms of prejudice are multi-layered. We recognize that racism is not just a belief that some race is superior or inferior, but exists at four different levels:

1. Internalized racism: As a result of socialization and education, individuals are conditioned to respond to, and generate, racist thoughts and images within themselves. This applies both to white people (who internalize the objectification or hatred

of other races) and to people of color (who internalize self-objectification and self-hatred).

Internalized racism does not have to be explicitly racist: most racists (white or POC) do not believe they are racist, and actually believe they are fair-minded people. This permits racism to continue to exist in society despite explicit racism being highly devalued.

2. Interpersonal racism: Individuals express their internalized racism to each other in passing comments, in conversation, in imagery, in articles, and so on. It's also expressed through the use of physical violence, all the way from harassment to hate crimes.

3. Institutionalized racism: Interpersonal racism becomes institutionalized when racist prejudice is expressed between individuals acting within an institution. Two examples of this would be discrimination in employment (within the workplace), and higher sentences for black offenders for the same crime (within the justice system).

4. Systemic racism: When racist attitudes or policies no longer solely apply within a given institution but also apply to people, situations, institutions or systems outside of that institution, we have what we would call a systemic or structural prejudice. Systemic prejudice demonstrates that the prejudice is not confined to personal beliefs or actions, but is ingrained in the very fabric of society. Racist

examples include police terrorist actions against black people, the Drug War, gentrification, real estate redlining, and immigration laws.

This framework can be applied to any prejudice, including childism, with the caveat that childism takes place within a narrower range of social relations (mostly the family structure and the education system). There is still internalized childism (internalized through socialization and schooling), interpersonal childism (mainly expressed by parents to their children or to other parents), institutionalized childism (within the family structure and the education system), and systemic childism (in the laws against abortion, in governments refusing to adequately provide for children's welfare, in sustaining the family structure and its omerta, in enforcing compulsory schooling, and so on).

More generally, we can say there are two basic elements to a prejudice: the actions that perpetuate its existence, and the beliefs and imagery which justify its existence. We can say that the latter corresponds roughly to points 1 and 2, while the former corresponds roughly to points 2, 3 and 4.

So we can say, for example, that sexism is the theory and misogyny/VAW is the practice, or that racism is the theory and discrimination/segregation/violence against POC is the practice. In the same way, childism is the theory and misopedia (child-hatred) is the practice.

Just as misogyny is reflected in all the ways men and women interact, misopedia is reflected in the myriad of ways in which adults interact with children, from the punishments I've listed above, the denial of basic human rights, the imposition of schooling, the stressful and dysfunctional nature of relations between children in school, the way children are portrayed in the media, the constant sexual harassment for girls, the particularly dismal treatment of children in religious sects, child poverty, the demonization of children who were labeled of a certain religion or race, and the way all of these different kinds of child-hatred are normalized.

Another area of similarity is in how some groups are made subordinate to others. In Letters from a War Zone, Andrea Dworkin lists four processes by which this is accomplished:

1. Hierarchy. There must be superior and inferior groups, such as men and women, whites and POC, adults (esp. parents) and children. These groups must be forced to interact with each other to some extent. In the case of childism, children have no choice but to deal with their parents on a constant basis, which means that their inferior status is reinforced at all times (in a similar way to women in heterosexual relationships, especially ones with children).

2. Objectification. A human being must be turned into something less than human, into a commodity. In objectification, the values and desires of the

person become irrelevant: they are reduced to some attributes, some body parts, a monetary value, etc. In the case of childism, the child is no longer a human being but the potential of a human being. As a mere potential, it has no rights but those which permit its development into a "successful" human being. Its values and desires are irrelevant, and it is reduced to its progress or lack of progress in becoming a "successful" human being (e.g. obedience, adherence to imposed social roles, good grades, a good college).

3. Submission. The inferior person must comply to the orders and desires of their (appropriate) superiors. In the case of childism, children must comply to the orders and desires of their parents, and it is generally assumed that adults are in a position of authority over children.

4. Violence. Inferiors are subject to systemic and endemic violence, and this violence is normalized by society. This is certainly true in the case of children, although not as much as in the past. Corporal punishment is now illegal in 46 countries, mostly in Europe and South America. Other Western countries allow the use of "reasonable" force on one's "own" child for the purpose of "discipline." Of course it is never asked how one could make the difference between "discipline" and assault, or what makes one physical assault on a child "reasonable" and another "unreasonable."

Another way to put childism within a prejudice framework is to look, not just at the stick (dictatorial control over one's life, physical, verbal and emotional abuse, forced self-identification, forced indoctrination, etc) but at the carrot. In The Culture of Conformism, Patrick Colm Hogan looks at the benefits that oppressed groups receive in exchange for their obedience, which he calls secondary gains:

> ... [T]here are two sorts of benefits that fall under the category of secondary gain. The first is purely negative. It is the benefit of not having to struggle for success thereby risking failure. The second benefit is positive and involves an attachment to any genuine advantages of the oppressed position.

In the case of negative secondary gains, Hogan discusses women being prevented from competing in mathematical or scientific fields, and in the case of positive secondary gains, he discusses women's exclusion from the military and courtship practices (such as men paying for dates).

Secondary gains are perhaps the most misunderstood aspect of prejudice. People often jump on benefits granted to oppressed groups as "proof" that they're not really being oppressed, and I expect childists will be no different, so the issue must be cleared up.

Children do receive secondary benefits for their obedience. They receive lodging, food, and (usually) support from their parents. They are not expected to contribute to most social institutions. These are huge benefits, but they are expected: after all, children need to be children and play with other children, not get involved in adult work.

Children do not, however, reap negative benefits. They are not in control of their own lives, but they are still held responsible for the failures of their parents' management of their lives. Parents do blame their children for being "undisciplined," even though this is really a failure on the part of the parents since "discipline" is seen as something imposed by the parents on the children. Society does impose poverty on children, even though that poverty is due to the parents, although it occasionally tries to mitigate that fact. A lack of proper education, psychological issues, lack of physical or emotional development due to parental failure, or poor genetics, are all left to the child, or later to the adult, to resolve for themselves.

In no case do children get a "free pass." The reason for this is obvious: children are emotionally and financially tied to their parents, so they are expected to be loyal. While children do occasionally run away, the issue of disloyal children is not really pressing. It is only when an oppressed group presents a very real political threat that the authorities will bother to throw them a bone, and children cannot be a political threat (or at least the kind of scenario needed for this to happen is so outlandish that it's not even worth thinking about).

Related to the concept of secondary gains is the

concept of weakness. I already quoted The Culture of Conformity on the infantile and adolescent models of childhood. Groups which are associated with the former (like, for example, goodly, pure women) gain the status of innocent victims, and automatically have the moral high ground. Women and children (and sometimes other groups) retain this status of being weak and in need of protection if they continue to conform to the infantile model: asexual, amoral, trusting, friendly, cute. Hurting them because a heinous crime, far beyond the scope of ordinary crimes.

This may seem like a benefit, but it's actually the result of prejudice (as we call it in the case of women, "putting women on a pedestal"). It is based on the premise that "good" women and children should accept the restrictions placed on them, and be unwilling to break the standards of "goodness." In exchange, they are to be protected to a greater extent than men and "bad" women and children (e.g. prostituted women, runaway children). Women and children generally get shorter prison sentences for the same crimes because they are seen as more innocent and in need of protection.

In her book Every Cradle is a Grave, Sarah Perry illustrates this point when she discusses how the traditional economic role of women and children underwent a sharp decline during the rise of capitalism, which meant that the Western world had to find a new role for women and children to occupy. The outcome was that women were reinvented as bearers of sacred motherhood, and children as innocent recipients of motherly love:

> Victorian concern for the well-being of children as a special, protected class is associated with the passage of laws regulating child labor and criminalizing abuse. Women gained status both from their newly-important role as mothers and from their new alliance with the church; they became guardians of virtue, and translated this into political power for child welfare causes.

Because childism is a prejudice similar to other prejudices, I think we can define it in a way similar to the way we define other prejudices. Based on that, the only issue I have with the two definitions I already gave is that they do not highlight the systemic nature of childism.

Usually, definitions of sexism and racism simply talk about discrimination or prejudice, but definitions of feminism and anti-racism inscribe prejudice within a larger social context. I find no particular reason for this bias: if being aware of prejudice means putting it in a larger social context, then why not define the prejudice itself as part of the social context? Based on this, I would define childism as:

Any prejudice against children based on "domestication" (i.e. based on the premise that children are "wild" and need to be "tamed"), especially that directed by parents against their children, or by other authority figures against children. This prejudice is ingrained in the family structure and, as a result, in the whole of society.

Before I continue, I do want to point out that there are certain differences between childism and other prejudices. All prejudices have their particularities, which derive from the social status and degree of social integration of their victims. Children are subjected to indoctrination by their parents and by other social institutions, indoctrination which they can hardly resist, partially because they are more physically dependent on outside help than any other group. Unlike any other discriminated group, they are forced by law to live with their oppressors. And unlike any other discriminated group in the Western world, they cannot participate in the political process.

These particularities do bleed over to other prejudices, like sexism and racism, because we were all once children. Childhood, unlike gender, race, disability, religion or class, is a universal experience. All women were once girls, and the gender socialization they received molded the way in which they deal with gender-based oppression. All black people were once black children, and the race socialization they received molded the way in which they deal with race-based oppression.

That being said, we may now ask, what is anti-childism? What does it involve? Like any other opposition to prejudice, it must start with the recognition that the childist prejudice is part of the institutions of our societies. It must also restore humanity to those people who have been dehumanized, made less-than-human. On this, let me quote David Kennedy, who is a professor in education and has written three books on childhood:

> I attribute to the child the same capacities, if not the same level or consistency of their realisation, for self-regulation and self-organisation that I find in or attribute to myself. I attribute to the child the same needs I find in myself: for autonomous action, for personal choice, for privacy, for respect from others, for personal exploration, for moments or periods of psychological regression, for nurturance, for meaningful work, for a reasonable level of power in the personal politics of the 'microsphere' or near environment, for leisure, for equal treatment in situations of dispute, for, in every case of conflict or failure, the recognition of mediating circumstances of one kind or another.[10]

Note that a lot of these points are reflected in the structure of Summerhill School, as well as the anti-pedagogical approach of Alice Miller, insofar as all pedagogies seek to suppress "autonomous action" and "equal treatment." Any parent who would treat their child in such a manner would be, at the very least, considered too "permissive."

And yet Kennedy is not saying anything that goes beyond the simplest precept of morality: treat others as you'd like to be treated. He is not arguing anything beyond the obvious: that children are human and therefore have human needs.

The anti-childist is seeking nothing more than the acknowledgement of children's humanity, just as the feminist seeks the acknowledgement of women's humanity and the anti-racist seeks to acknowledgement of POC's humanity.

Another document which seeks to establish the rights of children is the United Nations' Convention on the Rights of the Child. This document contains some interesting statements (bold mine):

> Article 12
>
> 1. States Parties shall assure to the child who is capable of forming his or her own views **the right to express those views freely in all matters affecting the child**, the views of the child being given due weight in accordance with the age and maturity of the child...
>
> Article 13
>
> 1. The child shall have **the right to freedom of expression**; this right shall include freedom to seek, receive and impart information and ideas of all kinds, regardless of frontiers, either orally, in writing or in print, in the form of art, or through any other media of the child's

choice...

Article 14

1. States Parties shall respect the right of the child to **freedom of thought, conscience and religio**n...

Article 18

1. States Parties shall use their best efforts to ensure recognition of the principle that both parents have common responsibilities for the upbringing and development of the child. Parents or, as the case may be, legal guardians, have the primary responsibility for the upbringing and development of the child. The **best interests of the child** will be their basic concern...

Article 24

1. States Parties recognize the **right of the child to the enjoyment of the highest attainable standard of health** and to facilities for the treatment of illness and rehabilitation of health. States Parties shall strive to ensure that no child is deprived of his or her right of access to such health care services...

All of these rights, which we would expect any adult human being to receive, are not being given to children: as a matter of fact, if these articles were followed exactly, the whole of society would be upended almost immediately. Article 24 alone would make abortion mandatory in some instances (as I will discuss in the chapter on abortion), since many pregnancies are known to result in children that will necessarily have poor health; if one gives birth to a child who will automatically have poor health, then where is that child's right to the highest attainable standard of health?

Reading article 18 literally, based on its specification that the best interests of the child should be the basic concern of parents or legal guardians, either entails a complete overhaul of the family structure, or its complete eradication. There is absolutely no way, under our current system, to ensure that parents act in anything remotely like the best interests of the child in mind.

Of course I don't expect that the people who wrote this Convention actually meant all these things literally. Since the document is very clearly pro-family structure, I don't expect it was meant to support abortion or the eradication of the family structure.

This shows the paradox of the liberal movement for "better child-raising": they simultaneously want to grant the children freedom and maintain the *status quo* as regards to the family structure, schooling, and religion. They still want to be free to procreate as much as they want, while trying to hold parents responsible for the children's well-being. If you look at it logically, you realize that something has to give. We can't continue to pretend to care about children as human beings while treating them as non-human objects of potential.

There is also another profound paradox in the concept of children's rights. As Western societies are products of the Enlightenment, we measure progress and maturity in terms of rationality and autonomy, amongst other standards, but we also view children as irrational and non-autonomous beings. This is why, no matter how much people try to protect children in a paternalistic manner similar to that of the United Nations document, they will remain unable to recognize the full humanity of children, as illustrated by the David Kennedy quote. Because he compared children to himself not based on adult standards (like education, rationality, maturity, independence, or status, all standards which necessarily exclude children) but on the actual capacities of children, Kennedy is able to realize the fundamental common humanity between himself and children.

As long as we adopt a paternalistic perspective based on adult standards as the only important standards of evaluation, we will never be able to recognize the full humanity of children, no matter how well intentioned we are. In a similar fashion, sexists and racists are unable to recognize the full humanity of women and people of color because they demand that they be evaluated on the basis of criteria established and maintained by males or whites (e.g. women are emotional, irrational, and ruled by their hormones, black people are lazy, unruly, and of inferior intelligence, and so on). This is no big mystery.

The main rationalizations for childism

All childism (and all objectification and exploitation, for that matter) starts from the premise that children are a means to an end. But children are human beings, and therefore should not be used as a means to an end. Rationalizations start from the fact that this basic premise must be buried, and buried deep, if the prejudice is to remain unopposed.

Rationalizations for prejudice are usually quite sophisticated. The rationalizations for racism and sexism have been refined for centuries and have faced a great deal of criticism. For these reasons, they tend to be pretty complicated. Childism, on the other hand, has not had to justify itself, so its rationalizations are still very simplistic. The three most important rationalizations of childism are:

* Children are not physically developed, therefore they are not mentally developed and are incapable of moral reasoning, decision-making, figuring out what's true and what's not, and so on.

* Children are dependent on adults for their survival, therefore children are inferior, therefore children must be controlled for their own good.

* Children are inherently gullible and believe anything their parents say, because evolution made

them that way.

Rationalizations, like all other lies, are more effective when there's some superficial truth behind them, and this is also true here. Children are physically developing, and they are dependent on adults to survive, so those two points are correct.

The third rationalization, however, simply has no truth behind it. Scientific studies have recorded epistemic distrust in children as young as 16 months old, and that by the time they are three years old they are able to outright reject demonstrably false claims (Clément, 2010). Children are not inherently gullible.

It is convenient for childists to believe that children are inherently gullible, because it hides the fact of children's condition. Very young children (1-5 years old) live in a closed environment, where they depend utterly on their parents. They have virtually no other sources of information than their parents. If their parents want to lie to them, they have little recourse.

Children are especially vulnerable to indoctrination. If parents wants to impose a religion, a political ideology, or any other belief system, there's little the children can do if it objects. Parents will withdraw affection and resources from children if they feel the latter aren't "getting with the program." There is little that a child can do in that situation but give in and start believing.

So the concept of child gullibility is actually a form of blaming the victim. Children are victims because they have no recourse against lies and indoctrinations. They have to believe what their parents tell them. And when we see a child talking about Santa Claus, we let ourselves have a self-indulgent chuckle at how gullible children are, even though those who lied to the child in the first place were adults like us.

It is also false to say that children cannot perform moral reasoning unless they are taught. Children as young as 12 months old help adults by pointing to the location of a displaced item, and children as young as 18 months old help adults at baby-accessible tasks[11]. Babies possess morality just as much as any adult, they just haven't yet learned the language necessary to formulate them.

Many call children "selfish," by which they mean that children are preoccupied only with their own well-being. But that is exactly as it should be! Children need to care about their own development, they don't need to care for other people. As A.S. Neill points out:

> Teachers from Israel have told me of the wonderful community centres there. The school, I'm told, is part of a community whose primary need is hard work. Children of ten, one teacher told me, weep if- as a punishment- they are not allowed to dig the garden. If I had a child of ten who wept because he was forbidden to dig potatoes, I

> should wonder if he were mentally defective. Childhood is playhood; and any community system that ignores that truth is educating in the wrong way...
>
> We must allow the child to be selfish- ungiving- free to follow his own childish interests through his childhood. When the child's individual interests and his social interests clash, the individual interests should be allowed precedence

Calling children selfish is wrong-headed. We would hardly call a cancer patient selfish for wanting more medical resources than the average person. Children need psychological and physical resources, and we owe it to them for having brought them into this world.

Apart from these points that are simply false, the three rationalizations have many others flaws. For instance, in each of these lines of reasoning, the conclusion is extremely specific: keep in mind that these are rationalizations used to justify the current family structure and current methods child-raising, with all the institutions that go along with them. This is an extremely specific and narrow conclusion. But the premises are all vague, general facts, like "children are dependent on adults" or "children are gullible." There's no way to start from vague general facts like this and get to such a specific conclusion.

You can compare this to Christian apologetics,

which is another form of rationalization. Their arguments also start from vague facts or pseudo-facts, like "there is design in the universe" or "objective morality exists" and end with the extremely specific conclusion that the Christian god, and no other god, exists and that his son is the only way to salvation. But, even if they were true, the premises could not support such specificity.

Anyone's agenda can fit into such vague premises. The argument from design can "prove" the existence of any god or gods you want, or extremely powerful aliens. Likewise, you could start from the premises given in the childist rationalizations and, with the same logic, argue all sorts of conclusions: that children should be raised in kibbutzim, in freedom schools, in tribes of hunter-gatherers, in monogamous heterosexual families, in polygamous or polyandrous families, or in authoritarian mind-bending cults.

Furthermore, we don't draw the same conclusion from other cases where human beings are dependent on other adults for their survival and are mentally under-developed or incapable of decision-making. One example is adults in a coma. Another is adults with mental disabilities. And yet we don't generally say that these two categories of adults are inferior to other adults, or justify total control over their lives on the basis of their dependence or physical issues.

Granted, the analogies are not perfect. Babies are more dependent on others than most adults with mental disabilities, and adults in a coma have no

99

(present) values or desires. Also, many bigots do believe that adults with mental disabilities are inferior (certainly the government of Nazi Germany thought so), but this belief is not grounded in any issue of dependence: it is generally based on some notion of normality or purity (genetic purity, racial purity) which is broken by the diminished capacities of such adults.

Now let's look at each rationalization in turn, starting with the one based on children not being physically developed. Of course it is true that children are not as physically developed as adults, but this does not prove that children are mentally inferior. A child is perfectly capable of moral reasoning, decision-making, and figuring out what's true and what's not, as long as these abilities are being applied to areas they know and care about. To measure a child on the basis of what adults know and care about makes as much sense as measuring adult intelligence on the basis of how much they understand quantum mechanics, or how good they are at speaking Basque.

Furthermore, even if children were mentally inferior, this would not prove that children must not have basic human rights. We don't do the same thing to mentally challenged adults, who are generally granted the same rights as other adults (although Texans seem to love executing them), even though they are generally seem as mentally inferior. Ethical considerations such as getting consent to act upon another person, not harming children, and not treating them as means to an end,

100

have more weight than a belief in someone's physical or mental inferiority.

The second rationalization is the one about dependency. Again, while it is true that children are dependent on others for their survival, it is not clear how this makes them inferior. We live in complex societies where we depend on each other for our food supply, clothes, health care, and other resources. We all depend on other people for our survival. Granted, this is more true in the case of children, but it doesn't exactly set them apart.

Is one person superior to another if they are able to provide more for themselves, such as growing their own food or making their own clothes, thus further lowering their dependency? While we may see this as a great set of skills to have, and a laudable lifestyle, it's not clear why that would make a person superior to others or more worthy of human rights.

The third rationalization pertains to gullibility. I've already explained why this is a false premise. But even if it was true, it's hard to understand how it could prove that children must be under the control of their parents. Actually, it seems to prove rather the opposite: if adults can easily bamboozle children, then maybe children should not be around adults so much, and with adults who have less power to indoctrinate them into believing all sorts of nonsense.

For most of us, our parents weren't the smartest or

most informed people in our lives. If we actually needed parenting because children need to be taught correctly, then only those most qualified to raise children would be parents. This is obviously not the situation we're in.

These rationalizations share one thing in common: they are perfect alibis for child abuse. Children's supposed stupidity and gullibility are used to obscure the reality of abuse. Children's dependency is used to coerce them into accepting abuse. And of course children's physical disadvantage makes abuse much easier for grown adults. Their role, in all cases, is to say: you shouldn't be on the side of the child because the child doesn't deserve credibility or consideration, and children are not worth defending. This is a powerful message, deeply ingrained in our culture, and one which I still fall into all too easily.

These are the main lines of rationalization used for childism. But we can look at rationalizations from another angle: they form layers of ideological defense, going from strongest to weakest. To take the example of gender, we find the following five layers:

1. Gender is innate.
2. Gender is so ingrained in the fabric of society that it cannot be eliminated.
3. Gender can be abolished, but the results would be catastrophic.
4. Gender can be abolished, but it would destroy individuality.

5. Abolishing gender is bigoted because it would go against people's self-identification.

Making the top layer credible is the most desirable outcome for supporters of the *status quo*. If the inferiority of some group is innate, then it is natural, inevitable, and it becomes desirable to accept it. After all, if women are innately inferior, or if POC are innately inferior, or if the workers are innately inferior, or if children are innately inferior, then there's no point in mucking about with society trying to enforce a futile equality between natural superiors (men, whites, the elite, adults) and natural inferiors (women, POC, workers, children).

Once you accept the prevalent "rational," "scientific" arguments presented for this natural inferiority (and there's never been any lack of such arguments: in the case of childism and gender at least, the arguments have been laid down all the way from Aristotle to today's quack neuroscientists), it makes perfect intellectual sense to be against equal rights. As Deborah Cameron writes in The Myth of Mars and Venus:

> [M]ost people are susceptible to the argument that if a difference between men and women has a biological basis, it is inevitable ('you can't argue with nature'), desirable ('what's natural is good'), and the world should be organized around it.

Likewise, a natalist might argue, as I've discussed above, that procreation is necessary because it's part of God's plan, or it's part of the evolutionary process and the purpose of our lives, or it's ingrained in our DNA, or some other nonsense. If that was true, then there would be no point in arguing against procreation.

At least, that's the argument. For many people, the conclusion makes sense, but from a logical standpoint it is not very persuasive: we know that many hierarchies that were previously believed to reflect innate inferiority, such as slavery (both ancient and modern), anti-semitism, monarchism, and various forms of gynocide (prostitution, war, witch-hunting, foot-binding, suttee death rituals, and so on), are now known to have been morally and factually wrong. Based on this, we can inductively conclude that it is likely that other supposed innate forms of inferiority will be disproved in the future as well (in many cases, such as gender and race, they are already disproved, but the disproof is not yet accepted by a majority of people).

The second and third layers have to do with social necessity instead of biological necessity. One may believe that a prejudice is not biologically justified but that it must exist in order for society to function in a moral or efficient way, although for most people they mainly represent a fallback position when the arguments based on biological necessity fail (as they inevitably will).

This is mostly the level at which religious fundamentalists are these days: since it's no longer viable to pretend that we're all innately religious, they like to bring out doom and gloom scenarios of what a totally secular world would look like, or the catastrophic consequences of abandoning this or that article of faith (the ones they seem to particularly like to prognosticate about are divine command theory, Christian Creationism, and free will, and what terrible woes will befall us if we abandon these beliefs).

The main difference between them is that the second layer is fatalistic, because it rests on the impossibility of change, while the third is not. As such, the second layer is not even a pretend appeal to truth, but can be an appeal to force or an appeal to authority, depending on how it's formulated. For instance, someone faced with an anti-procreation argument might say things like:

"Any movement trying to limit procreation would be suppressed, so there's no point in trying."
"The position for procreation is so credible, and so many great thinkers agree with it, that nothing you can say will change anything."

Neither of these statements would address the actual argument, or any truth about procreation itself. But, like all other layers, it does serve the purpose of trying to end the discussion and block any further possibility of discussion. And I think this is pretty persuasive with people: if there's no possibility of solving a problem, most people will choose to rationalize or deny the problem. In folk philosophy, fatalism is inextricably linked to passivity and

105

silence: there's no point to talking about things that cannot change, one must simply accept them.

This may seem like a convincing line of reasoning until one goes back to the hierarchies I discussed above. Centuries ago, many people would no doubt have said that they would continue unabated forever, and that it was unrealistic to expect that, for example, slavery, while still a pressing ongoing concern, would ever be illegal in all the countries of the world. It might have been mind-boggling for someone living in the Middle Ages to imagine most monarchies either ceasing to exist or be converted to constitutional monarchies. Many opponents of slavery or monarchy no doubt felt that they were fighting an impossible battle. And yet, from our perspective, they clearly were not.

Because of that, one might make an inductive argument that claims of social necessity must be viewed with extreme suspicion. If institutions as ancient and solid as slavery and monarchism could be discredited to the extent they are today (and keep in mind that these institutions were justified through biological necessity as well), then there's no particular reason to believe that existing hierarchies will continue to exist forever to the extent that they do today.

The third layer is more akin to the slippery slope fallacy, which consists of positing that if one bad thing happens (bad, of course, from their perspective), then other even worse things must inevitably happen. If we allow homosexuals to marry, then polygamists will be able to get married, and then people will be able to marry other animals, and then objects. This becomes an appeal to fear when the slippery slope reaches its fullest extent.

This sort of argument is often used against people who do not punish their children, and also against free education. Against the latter, it is usually argued that a free education is inherently inferior and will lead to "our country" falling behind in science and mathematics. Here is a particularly egregious example:

> When your competitors are insisting that their children master higher mathematics, to the exclusion of many of the fun aspects of childhood, you are not doing your children any favors.
>
> Your well-rounded fun-loving creative child will not be able to compete against a cohort that has mastered multivariable calculus and convex optimization.

There is definitely a racist element here (who are these "competitors" and "cohorts" who are math wizards if not stereotypical Asians?), but the important element is the slippery slope. Because pedagogy and coerced education are supposed to turn children into productive and "successful" citizens, people conclude that abandoning pedagagy or coerced education will turn a population into unproductive, frivolous, stupid people who cannot do mathematics or science. Never mind that there's no evidence that pedagogy or coerced education actually does turn children into more productive or "successful" citizens than their opposite, or improves mathematical or scientific skills.

Related to this is the fear of role reversal. It is one of the obsessions of the privileged to prevent their inferiors from taking over and punishing them for their transgressions. The fear of role reversals is part of all the prejudices you care to look at, and has always had some place in Western culture (see for example Saturnalia, the Feast of Fools, and mumming). Racists see anti-racist theory as calling for the extermination of white people. Misogynists associate the end of the patriarchy with women controlling society. Capitalists associate anarchism with mob violence and nihilistic destruction. Childists associate the idea of giving children freedom with children controlling adults and running amok.

The fourth and fifth layers have to do with self-image and self-identification. Once a system of prejudice is in place, people come to grasps with their position in the hierarchy: through constant conformity to the requirements of that position and the gains one accrues from them (whether primary or secondary), they come to identify with their position, and the hierarchy upon which their gains depend. So the irony here is that the indoctrination which results from the imposition of a prejudice is then used to "prove" that the prejudice is necessary for people's mental well-being. This is little more than a circular argument.

These layers don't really apply to childism as much as they apply to other prejudices, which are used as ways to self-identify, although one can anticipate perhaps future objections to child freedom formulated in that vein: "you just want to treat children like adults" and so on. Obviously this would be a misguided objection: equality of rights and freedoms does not mean we should treat everyone the same way. It's clear that people have different needs and abilities, and that treating everyone the same would be unfair. Children have developmental needs specific to children, which must be accounted for.

We can rephrase these layers to examine childist rationalizations (removing the fifth layer, for the reason I just pointed out):

1. Children's inferiority is innate.
2. Childism is so ingrained in the fabric of society that it cannot be eliminated.
3. Childism can be abolished, but the results would be catastrophic.
4. Childism can be abolished, but it would destroy individuality.

Right now, the childist rationalizations (including the three I've given) are firmly rooted in the first layer, and this, I think, is because childism hasn't yet been challenged at any substantial level, only at its periphery (corporal punishment, exploitation of children's sexuality and labor, severe or lethal mistreatment of children by their parents). There has not yet been any public questioning on the status of children, not even in some vague undefined way, no small but vocal group bringing up points either in online communities or in the real world, as far as I am aware of.

So childism has not yet been challenged to the point where it would have to fall back to any other layer of rationalization. In the absence of opposition strong enough to knock it down, a prejudice will inevitably remain on its highest and most stable platform, which is that of biological necessity.

Before I end this section, let me list the three main rationalizations again:

* Children are not physically developed, therefore they are not mentally developed and are incapable of moral reasoning, decision-making, figuring out what's true and what's not, and so on.

* Children are dependent on adults for their survival, therefore children are inferior, therefore children must be controlled for their own good.

* Children are inherently gullible and believe anything their parents say, because evolution made them that way.

Here I want to point out that these rationalizations are really extensions of natalism, that is to say, they serve to objectify and dehumanize children. We understand ourselves, as humans, to be distinct from other species on the basis of our moral reasoning, decision-making and ability to discover truths (the validity of this understanding is another issue entirely). In the Western world, where capitalism is dominant, we value our lives only insofar as we can be independent (being a burden on others is one of the most reliable predictors of suicide).

Insofar as we understand childhood to be the opposite of these two things, we will naturally devalue it and dehumanize it. And this makes possible the objectification of children that we observe in natalism. If children are outside what we consider "fully human," and do not have valuable lives except as potential for the future, then we have no reason to take their needs and desires into account when promoting procreation as a solution for economic or social ills. The easiest way to objectify others is to believe that "they don't think like we do."

This relationship is only exacerbated by the fact that our societies are geared towards following natalist principles. All institutional prejudices are self-fulfilling, insofar as institutions structured around them will inevitably bring about the outcome that is being preached as "natural" and "necessary." A society where children are believed to be potential human beings instead of actual human beings, and where institutions are structured to follow the logical consequences of that belief, will produce children who are trained to obey authority, whose independence has not been cultivated, and who have little critical thinking skills or self-determination

The supposed right to procreate

There is little disagreement in the world about the fact that most, or all, human beings have a right to procreate: there exists only mild disagreement about the limit cases. For the most part, there is no dissent whatsoever on any issue related to this right. The right to procreate is considered "fundamental" by the United States Supreme Court and the United Nations. There is a great deal more debate on reproductive rights, including the right to abortions and contraception, but there is general agreement (except in China, obviously) that anyone who wants to produce children, no matter how many, should be free to do so.

Despite their fights over various reproductive rights, this is one of the many things that conservatives and liberals agree on: that procreation in itself is a social good and that abortions should be as few as possible. We should not be surprised that advocates of the *status quo* are also, if not outright natalists, at least sympathetic to natalist aims. After all, natalism is all about maintaining existing structures of power against the threat of lowered birth rates. Patriotism and natalism have always existed hand-in-hand.

However, we should consider claims of procreation being a fundamental human right with great suspicion. Obviously a natalist would see procreation as being a human right, since, from the natalist perspective, the needs and desires of women and children are already out of the equation. Given the widespread suffering that procreation entails for these two categories of people, a wider, more objective, perspective on the issue is needed.

The concept of human rights is a vast one, used to describe many different things. Here I want to focus on one specific conception, that of universal principles of ethics. Human rights, as we generally understand them, have as aim to prevent people from being harmed, especially in situations of profound inequality, such as that which prevails between one individual and a government or corporation. Notable enumerations of rights, such as the Magna Carta, the Universal Declaration of Human Rights, and bills and charters of rights written into various constitutions, are all primarily limitations on the power that governments exert over their free citizens (women, children, and natives have only recently begun to be counted as free, and usually didn't count at all).

For the sake of precision, I should mention that I am not endorsing any particular conception of human rights, and I have much disagreement with the documents I've listed. I am merely looking at the way people generally conceive of human rights.

But governments are not the only parties who are limited by human rights. Take for example the right to freedom of association, a right which has been rather violently suppressed by corporations, and continues to be suppressed in various ways. Or the right to freedom of thought which, as I've pointed out, is massively and profoundly violated by the continued existence of the family structure. The common thread in these instances is, again, profound inequality.

There is no greater inequality in this world than the inequality between a parent and a child. It seems therefore rather curious that parents are granted a right to procreate. In one way, it is understandable: States have, at various times, sought to sterilize populations as a form of eugenics or genocide (such as the attempt by the United States government to exterminate Native Americans during the 1970s). This was wrong, procreative rights or no, because it was done without consent or with incomplete consent.

For most people, this will be the end of the reasoning. There is no reason to bring up children, because children are not human beings and therefore do not have rights.

However, if we start from the premise that children are human beings and have rights, we then must raise the question: what about the child's rights? A right can hardly be a right if its exercise harms other people. We don't recognize the right to free speech when the speech harms others (through fraud, threats, the depiction of criminal activities, and so on). We don't recognize the right to marry in the case of polygamy, because polygamous relationships are predicated on women's inferiority (so are all marriages, for that matter, but we blithely ignore that fact, stick our fingers in our ears and sing real loud, in the name of social stability and tradition).

Although there are generally no laws against it, we commonly believe that a pregnant woman should not smoke, drink alcohol, or use drugs. We know that such actions can engender bad health outcomes for the future child. We've all heard of crack babies and fetal alcohol syndrome. If children have rights, then surely one of the most important rights they have is the right to be born healthy and remain as healthy as possible. Being born as a crack baby or with fetal alcohol syndrome is a direct contradiction of that right.

It is clearly not the case that a woman has the right to willfully start a life that she has compromised, because that would mean that she has the right to bring harm to another person, which is a contradiction.

You may argue that this represents more of an exception to the right to procreate than a contradiction: after all, most pregnant women don't smoke, drink alcohol, or use drugs. But why would we draw the line here? There is always a risk of certain genetic defects. What about children who are born with Down's Syndrome or congenital heart defects, for instance? You can argue that the woman had no intent of having a child compromised in these ways, but it's undeniable that the woman had the intent of having a child with these risks clearly known.

If we have no right to start a compromised life, then

115

logically we also have no right to put people under the risk of starting their lives compromised; this is merely an extension of the general principle that if any act is wrong, then willfully putting someone at risk of being acted upon in that way must also be wrong.

Children may also grow up into adults whose health may become compromised, often partially for genetic reasons. They may be deprived of sound health for the rest of their lives through no fault of their own. Do these adults, also, not have rights?

What about cases where abusive parenting or parental neglect collude with genetics to create mental health problems in the child? We blame teenagers (who we classify as impure, rebellious creatures) who resort to cutting, drugs or sex to deal with their mental distress, but we never stop to ask who caused it. Should not parents be held accountable for that, too? If despair was an identifiable, tangible, transmissible disease, we would no more support its forced transmission than we support people who give others HIV without their consent.

This brings me to one inexorable conclusion: if the so-called right to procreate entails breaking numerous fundamental rights of children, and children are human beings, then there can be no such thing as a right to procreate.

And that's not to speak of other reproductive rights. If we have no right to have children, then obviously we have no right to decide how many children to have, or the timing of those births, or whether or not to have an abortion. All those other issues fall by the wayside, once we reject the "right to procreate."

As Daniel Mackler, a follower of Alice Miller's ideology, rightly states:

> The basic human right is the right of the child to be born to parents who will love him fully, attend to all his needs, and not torture him with the neglect that is our modern world's standard—and the standard of our modern world to deny. Stopping people from torturing their future offspring trumps the inappropriate parental desire—that is, "right"—to procreate.

Note the phrasing here: not "a human right," not "a basic human right," but "**the** basic human right." It is the only basic, fundamental human right, because it is from childhood that the person develops their capacities, including the capacities relevant to their rights (including physical and mental health, the means to live, free expression, justice, and ultimately the pursuit of happiness). The expression of all other human rights, without exception, depends upon the right of the child to have their needs fulfilled in childhood.

The argument I discussed earlier regarding freedom of thought applies equally to all other rights. It makes no more sense to say that a child who was indoctrinated into one or the other religion for 18 years is suddenly free to believe anything they want. And it makes equally no sense to say that a child who was not treated with the highest standard of physical or mental health for 18 years suddenly has the right to "life, liberty and the pursuit of happiness," when we are all to some extent damaged from our childhood and are partially or completely unable to pursue these lofty goals.

I want to make clear that I am not just talking about the extreme cases of child abuse here. If that was the case, then it would be easy to see them as exceptions to the "right to procreate": just stop the "really bad parents" (the child-beating fundamentalists, the anti-vaccination advocates, the police and military wife-beaters, and so on) from procreating and leave the rest to it. My point is that any damage from childhood, even if it is not extreme, is a direct attack on our human rights as adults.

Unless there is some prejudice involved, we don't think it a justification of someone's action that they merely pushed someone into a wall instead of stabbing them: either way, it's a form of assault and it's reprehensible. The degree to which an adult's human rights are attacked by their childhood damage should not be important. A supposed right which can be taken away to any degree is not really a right to begin with.

One more area in which the "right to procreate" can easily be shown to cause harm, and therefore not being an actual right, is in the way procreation causes harm to society and mankind. Every single new human being put on this planet creates a burden of harm on everyone else, in the form of using resources that could have been used for other purposes, in the form of imposing harm on others to transform those resources so they can be consumed, and in the form of pollution throughout the process.

If you are an environmentalist, you should know that nothing you do, personally or as a group, to "save the planet" measures up to the harm you do by having just one child. The average person in the world generates 4 metric tons of carbon dioxide a year through transportation and home energy use alone, but the average for industrial nations, which I assume most of my readers are from, is 11 tons a year (and the American average is 20 tons, cue the obesity jokes here). Contrast this with some popular green measures, like eating vegetarian (saves 2.5 tons a year), recycling your newspapers (saves 184 pounds a year), bringing your own bags to the grocery store (saves 17 pounds a year), or planting a tree (saves 25 pounds a year).

My point is not that you should not be doing these things. If you do, all the better! But if you also have a child, then all your efforts are in vain: anything you do will have little influence compared to the huge negative you've introduced. And if your child decides to have children down the line, then their pollution is on your hands as well.

We spend hundreds of billions of dollars around the world raising up children. These dollars translate into actual resources used to manufacture throwaway diapers, clothes that will be discarded yearly, baby toys, carriers, seats, blankets, and of course baby food. This is an enormous mass of resources which could be used to help the people who are already here.

The truth is that we have no choice on whether to subsidize the welfare and education of new human lives. We must accept other people's procreation as a given, beyond the possibility of discussion, even though we did not consent to its effects on our society. Now I am not saying that we should not subsidize the welfare and education of children; obviously we must do so, not for the parents' sake but for the children's sake. The children are not responsible for this state of affairs, and do not deserve to be punished for it.

As for the harm imposed on others in the production of these goods, it's important to remember that slavery and sweatshops still exist, and that slave labor and sweatshop labor are intricately involved in the manufacture of the goods we buy. Many of these slaves and sweatshop workers are children. And we're not even talking about the mistreatment of workers here at home, which is another story entirely.

Each and every one of us is responsible for inflicting harm on others in order to live modern, comfortable Western lives. I am not trying to make you feel guilty: you didn't ask to be born in a Western country. But to give birth to a child, knowing all these things, is an unconscionable act. To say that we have a right to do so means that we have the right to generate suffering on a massive scale, which is an absurd proposition.

But these facts are not salient to people who have children. And why should they be? Natalist propaganda tells you about the good parts, but omits all of the bad parts. Sure, they'll tell you how great it is to be a parent, to raise your own children, and for some people that does work out well; many people are not cut out to be parents, and for them having children becomes a living hell, but they never talk about that.

Insofar as social impact is concerned, the natalist party line is just as biased. The argument that having more children will lead to better economic outcomes is based on a narrow-minded view of economic progress as the production and consumption of more goods, the creation of new technology without care for their impact, and the bigoted insistence that one's country must remain on par or superior to others in these categories.

This view, oriented towards corporate profits and mindless patriotism, serves only the interests of the power elite. Natalism furthers the *status quo*. There is nothing more traditional and conventional than to praise people for having children. In contrast, the points I've raised here are about how natalism negatively affects everyone living on this planet, in some way or another.

There is one support of the "right to procreation" which I must address because it comes from a famous antinatalist, philosopher David Benatar, author of the seminal book on antinatalism Better Never to Have Been. In chapter 4 of that book, he argues that even though having children is clearly wrong, we should still grant people "reproductive rights" because of the consequences:

> [T]he argument in defence of a legal right to reproductive freedom might go, procreative prohibition simply would not work. People would find ways of breaking the law. To enforce the law, even partially and unevenly, the [S]tate would have to engage in highly intrusive policing and the invasions of privacy that that would entail... The threat of [unwanted abortions] would very likely drive pregnancy underground, with women gestating and giving birth on the quiet. This, in turn, would very likely increase pregnancy- and parturition-related morbidity and mortality. These sorts of moral costs are immense...

It's hard not to see the analogy Benatar is making between back-alley abortions resulting from an anti-abortion policy and back-alley pregnancies resulting from a pro-abortion policy. This is a fair point, but it does not prove the existence of a legal right. Likewise, alcohol prohibition did not work and thousands of people died because of it, but this alone does not prove we have a right to be drunk, or to drive drunk. It's entirely possible for an act to be harmful and for its prohibition to also be harmful.

My point here is not that we should "balance" the benefits and the harms of each position. As I'll argue later, such a "balancing" is logically impossible and therefore pointless. We should strive to prevent people from harming each other. Obviously, any solution to harm that involves harming people is equally pointless.

Benatar's problem is that he thinks the only alternative to recognizing a right to procreate is violent suppression. But this is silly: no right or freedom to make origami is enshrined in any constitution or document, and yet we don't go around violently preventing people from folding paper. A more sensible alternative to the belief in a "right to procreate" would be to end all economic incentives towards having children, make childfreedom a more desirable social status, and remind people of the enormous harm that having children inflicts on the planet.[12]

The family structure

The family structure is an institution which we roughly define as single individuals, or couples in monogamous heterosexual (although this requirement is changing) relationships usually sealed by marriage, who raise children in a closed environment (the family home). This implies a number of institutional supports, such as property rights, privacy rights, heteronormativity, the

123

existence of marriage or other exclusive relationships, and so on.

Many people still believe that the purpose of marriage is procreation. While this may not ring true today in the Western world, given the widespread acceptance of homosexuality and the rise of childfreedom, it certainly reflects historical reality. Marriage served the purpose of controlling procreation through the sexual ownership of women. Nowadays we prefer to impose mutual sexual ownership. Either way, the control over procreation is still the end point of marriage. Homosexuals and the childfree are free riders of an institution which was not designed for them (not that I think that's a bad thing).

The family is a hierarchy, and this hierarchy is simple: parents are at the top and their children are at the bottom. I've pointed out that this hierarchy is extreme in its power disparity. But I will go further here and say that parents have ownership over their children.

I realize this is a particularly controversial claim. When people think of a human being owning another, they automatically think of slavery. While I don't think that most children are treated with the level of abuse that the concept of slavery summons in our imagination, the concept of human ownership does not necessarily have to entail slavery.

Consider the concept of "child poverty." This is a normalized concept which does not surprise anyone.

We hear about it all the time. However, if you start looking at the logic of it, you will quickly twist yourself into knots of illogic. According to the prevalent capitalist worldview, good investments and needed work must be rewarded, and bad investments and unfruitful work must be punished, in order to provide the incentive needed for "the economy" to progress (what we call the Invisible Hand). Poverty is a punishment meted out to those people who are too lazy or too stupid to adequately meet the demand.

Now, we know this is not an even remotely adequate model of reality. But even if we assume the validity of this model, child poverty makes no sense whatsoever. Babies can't make investments or work. Babies can't "meet demand." And yet some of them are "rich" and some of them are "poor."

The reason is obvious: children are rich or poor in accordance with their family's economic status. The well-being of a child is directly related to the well-being of its parents. The fact that their parents must be punished entails that they must also be punished, because children, for all intents and purposes, are owned by their parents.

What does it mean to own a human being[13] ? It means that the human being that is owned has no input in their own lives except through the charity of the owner, and becomes basically an object with little to no rights. This is the situation of children in a family structure: until they attain adult age, they have no input in their own lives except through the charity of their parents, and they have little rights.

The main difference, of course, is that parents generally love their children and most parents do not deliberately seek to exploit their children, because they do not need their children's labor to survive as they did in the past. This is a vast improvement in children's condition. However, it does not nullify the facts at hand. A kind and gentle dictator is still a dictator.

My use of the word "dictator" is not accidental. The family structure is totalitarian in nature. Soviet writer Fazil Iskander wrote that "[under a] totalitarian regime, it was as if you were forced to live in the same room with an insanely violent man." Children whose parents were violent or verbally abusive know exactly how that feels: they lived under such a totalitarian regime for their entire childhood, and there is no private space for such a child any more than there is under a totalitarian regime.

Mary Astell makes a good point in her book Some Reflections Upon Marriage:

> If Absolute Sovereignty be not necessary in a State, how comes it to be so in a Family? or if in a Family why not in a State; since no Reason can be alledg'd for the one that will not hold more strongly for the other?

Granted, her point was about women, not children, but the point remains relevant.

Because of the extreme power imbalance between parents and children, and the fact that we are all damaged by childhood, the parents are in an ideal situation to reproduce the abuse they were subjected to, because it was sold to them as normal and a sign of love, and to relieve the frustrations that came from that abuse. Alice Miller calls this the *repetition compulsion* and explains this process in For Your Own Good:

> 1. For parents to be aware of what they are doing to their children, they would also have to be aware of what was done to them in their own childhood. But this is exactly what was forbidden them as children. If access to this knowledge is cut off, parents can strike and humiliate their children or torment and mistreat them in other ways, without realizing how they are hurting them; they simply are compelled to behave this way.
>
> 2. If the tragedy of a well-meaning person's childhood remains hidden behind idealizations, the unconscious knowledge of the actual state of affairs will have to assert itself by an indirect route. This occurs with the aid of the repetition compulsion. Over and over again, for reasons they do not understand, people will create situations and establish relationships in which they torment or are tormented by their partner, or both.
>
> 3. Since tormenting one's children is a

legitimate part of child-rearing, this provides the most obvious outlet for bottled up aggression.

4. Because an aggressive response to emotional and physical abuse is forbidden by parents in almost all religions, this outlet is the only one available.

Note that, for the most part, parents do not understand that what they are doing to their children is abusive and a consequence of their own abuse. Because they grew up believing that it was a form of love, they do it to their own children because they love them and they believe that's how parental love works.

The repetition compulsion does not only apply to the parent-child relationship: the family structure just happens to be the ideal means to express it. Other relationships, such as between lovers, boss and employee, cop and citizen, and between other authority figures and ordinary people, also provide an opportunity for repetition to be expressed, although the victims in those cases are more likely to resist and assert their rights. It is precisely the extreme inequality between parents and children that makes the family structure the ideal framework for expressing the repetition compulsion.

The family structure and the schooling system make the objectification manifested in natalist thought plausible. The main result of all the indoctrination that is part of both systems is to produce conformity and competitiveness, and it makes it a lot easier to objectify people if those people actually do behave more like objects than like human beings. So the objectification is actually a self-fulfilling prophecy: we set up institutions which are based on the premise that children are objects serving an economic and social purpose, and then we use the end result of those institutions (conformist children who have been stamped with the urgency of becoming economic and social agents) to justify the premise that children are objects serving an economic and social purpose.

Belief in the family structure is predicated on the belief that any two random people who are able to have sex are also competent enough to raise children in a structure that basically invites abuse. This belief is bolstered by the life blueprint: if having children and raising them is one of the things everyone should do in order to be normal, then it must be the case that anyone can raise children. To say otherwise would mean to deny that some people can be happy, just because of a lack of certain skills, and this would be pretty cruel.

But if we're being realistic about this, we should admit that the only thing most people know about raising children is the way they were raised, and little to nothing more. Furthermore, they have a vested interest in closing their eyes to the ways in which their parents raised them badly. No one wants to blame their parents, for obvious reasons.

The simple fact is that most parents are not

qualified to raise children. And we know this because we already have standards for child care: those imposed on people who work in, well, child care. Standards for child care workers vary by region, but generally require the absence of a criminal record, a secondary school/high school diploma, babysitting experience, and, especially for higher positions, some sort of government permit or a diploma in child education (in some places, only the first two are required).

How many parents have these qualification? Except, obviously, child care workers, I would wager that most do not, especially if you consider that being the parent of a child is such a complete responsibility that it would hardly do to measure parents on the standard of a daycare assistant. If parents have to do it all, then they should be qualified to do it all. If we establish requirements for childcare workers because we're worried about the way children are treated while under someone else's care, then why are we not worried about the way children are treated in their own homes?

The idea of a parental licence is not a new idea, and I will come back to it in the last chapter. But for now, it will suffice to say that the family structure puts people in charge of raising children on a purely arbitrary basis (that is, except if we see it as an ownership relation), not on the basis of ability to raise children in a healthy manner. This has consequences, and we see these consequences on a daily basis: much of the self-destruction and destruction of others we see in our societies stem from the inability to deal with childhood trauma.

Anyone reading this may accuse me of having a bleak view of the family structure, and perhaps blame my own upbringing. Actually, my own upbringing was very free, as far as upbringings go. Psychologically, it is adults who were the most abused in childhood who find the need to defend their parents, as Alice Miller's work has demonstrated. I am not here to defend or attack anyone, merely to state the facts of the case.

I think many people would bring up the "bad apples" rhetoric as an answer to all that I've said in this section: that while there may be some "bad parents" out there who are dictatorial, most parents are reasonable and have no intention of being dictators. But this would be an error, since nothing I said has to do with "bad parents" as opposed to "good parents." My criticism is not a criticism of any individual, not of my parents, or your parents, but of the institution itself.

Institutions are not just a loose group of people who make up rules as they go. Institutions have histories, ideological backing, rules and regulations, incentive systems, and so on. The latter is perhaps most important here: the very existence of an institution entails the existence of incentive systems which mold individual behavior. What this means is that no matter how good or bad people are, they will still conform to the incentives given to them.

The things I've discussed so far, such as the fact of

child ownership, the extreme power imbalance, the objectification of natalism, and the lack of qualifications of most parents, are all inherent to the institution itself, and do not change whether the parents are "good parents" or "bad parents." While "bad parents" are more likely to uses these incentives to harm their children, all parents are subject to them.

Again, the institution of slavery may cast some light on this phenomenon. Kind slaveowners were not unknown, and they believed themselves to be caring people. But, from our place in history, we now see clearly that slavery itself was the injustice, not cruel masters. All slaveowners could have been angels of mercy, and this still would not have made the institution of slavery (i.e. the ownership of another human being based on capitalist logic) morally good.

I have previously discussed the family structure as an extreme form of hierarchy. All hierarchies comes with specific problems. In the book Top Down, Harold Leavitt, while arguing that hierarchies are necessary (a position I disagree with, but which is beyond the scope of this book), identifies a number of major problems with hierarchical organizations:

1. They generate childlike dependency.
    In human hierarchies, some people, by design, have more power than others, so those having less power become, to varying degrees, dependent on those having more.

2. They mistreat their inferiors.
>We don't like big organizational hierarchies because they make working people unwilling serfs of stupid or wicked bosses. They shackle us to dull, repetitive routines. They discourage imagination. They quash creativity. They treat us capriciously. They make us do useless things. They don't really trust us, either.

3. They block warm interpersonal relationships.
>Hierarchies are forever preaching about the importance of teamwork. But although they urge cooperation, they reward competition.

4. They breed greed and immorality.
>Hierarchies give some people great power, power that tends to build on itself. Eventually that power is likely to corrupt.

5. They're inefficient.
>[S]nowballs of misinformation are commonplace in large hierarchies. They grow, distort, and accelerate as they roll down bureaucratic pyramids.

6. They violate democratic values.
>Large organizations' inescapable need for hierarchy, and therefore for authority, clashes with egalitarian values of democratic societies.

And to these I would add at least one more point:

7. They lack accountability.
> The greater the inequality of power between superiors and inferiors, the less recourse inferiors have when they are mistreated.

All the points by Leavitt are written with corporations in mind, but most of them apply with even more power to the family structure (except for point 5, which is specific to large hierarchies):

1. Saying that the family structure generates "childlike dependency" may seem a little ironic, given that the inferiors, in this case, are actual children. Children are dependent on resources and support, but they can also have the freedom to develop independence. In a family structure, children do not, and cannot, have that freedom, by definition. They cannot work out how to live in society with other children their age, as equals, instead of being subordinates for the first 18 years of their lives.

Therefore we can truly say that the family structure does even worse than generating a healthy "childlike dependency," which at least would incorporate elements of growth and independent thought as well The best we can say is that the family structure generates unhealthy and dysfunctional "childlike dependency."

2. As I'll discuss in the section on the "childist omerta," the family structure creates the possibility for virtually unlimited abuse. Most parents do not attain such a level of abuse, but most parents still

think that physical, verbal and emotional abuse are acceptable means of keeping children "in line." In any other context, we'd decry such means as absurd.

3. Much has been made of parents encouraging competition between siblings. But that form of competition is nowhere nearly as powerful as the competition in the outside world that parents are trying to "adapt" their children to. In essence, the biggest form of competition within the family structure is that which takes place between families. Big or small, poor or rich, religious or non, all families compete with each other for the "success" of their children, and all children are competing against each other for the best education and the best jobs. Instead of uniting people with common interests, children, the family structure pits them against each other.

This serves an important "divide and conquer" purpose in that it prevents children from realizing their class interests. They identify with their family and analyze the world based on their own personal interests, instead of identifying with fellow children and analyzing the world in a systemic manner.

4. If power corrupts, then being a parent must turn you into a corrupted human being. What do we mean when we say a politician or CEO is corrupt? I think we mean that the individual has stopped seeing other people as ends-in-themselves, and instead uses other people as a tool to generate profit or power. But this process is built into the very nature of the family structure: the alignment

paradigm entails that parents will not treat their children as ends-in-themselves, but rather as potential adults. Parents, insofar as they are being parents, are corrupt by definition.

5. This point applies to large organizations, so it doesn't really apply to individual families. It does, however, apply to some extent to the family structure as a whole: having children be raised individually or in small groups (depending on the family) is probably much more inefficient than raising them in communities, in terms of manpower, money spent, and the gigantic quantity of productive work that parents could have done if they hadn't been parents. Obviously I have no numbers to give due to the complexity of the issue, but it's a point to consider.

6. Violating democratic values is one of the basic principles of the family structure: any system that acknowledged the rights and self-determination of children would look nothing like it.

7. Parents have a minimum level of accountability to the State, insofar as committing a crime against their children may get the State to take their children away or to put them in jail. But parents have no accountability to their children and are not held accountable for harming the health or well-being of their children in a non-criminal manner.

Because the family structure is such an extreme form of hierarchy, and hierarchies cause so much harm by their very existence, I follow the principle, espoused by Noam Chomsky, that we should reject *all* hierarchies unless rational justification is provided for their existence. This is an important point, so let me quote his book Understanding Power on this principle:

> [T]he basic principle I would like to see communicated to people is the idea that every form of authority and domination and hierarchy, every authoritarian structure, has to prove that it's justified- it has no prior justification. For instance, when you stop your five-year-old kid from trying to cross the street, that's an authoritarian situation: it's got to be justified. Well, in that case, I think you can give a justification. But the burden of proof for any exercise of authority is always on the person exercising it- invariably. And when you look, most of the time these authority structures have no justification: they have no moral justification, they have no justification in the interests of the person lower in the hierarchy, or in the interests of other people, or the environment, or the future, or the society, or anything else- they're just there in order to preserve certain structures of power and domination, and the people at the top.

We can justify things like stopping a five year old from crossing the street (which, by the way, does not justify the family structure: there's nothing about being a parent that makes you more able to protect a child from getting run over), or, say, firefighters having the right to break windows or doors to put out a fire, or emergency vehicles being able to double park. In these examples, the interventions are rooted in fact and there are obvious benefits for *everyone involved* beyond "maintaining a certain distribution of power." It would be mendacious at best, even for a committed egalitarian and anti-hierarchy person like myself, to complain about any of these things.

But when we look not just at a narrow range of specific actions which serve some justifiable purpose, but rather at entire institutions, we end up in the category of unjustified hierarchies most of the time. Those hierarchies serve a purpose, but there's no particular reason to believe that we need those specific hierarchies to serve that purpose, and therefore the harms that those hierarchies inflict remains unjustified.

In our Western societies, we happen to believe in the necessity of the family structure: this is a conditional belief (i.e. its existence is dependent on other conditions), as demonstrated by the fact that other societies do not necessarily share it.

The purpose of the family structure is to raise children, provide for them, and prepare them for adulthood. These purposes are entirely necessary. This does not, however, prove that the family structure is necessary, because the purpose could be fulfilled in a number of different ways. For example, parents could raise children up to age 6 and then send them to a freedom school until their adulthood. Or we could abandon the ridiculous idea that copulation is an indicator of child-rearing skills, and have children raised by skilled professionals up to age 6 instead. Or children could be raised by a group of people, or by the entire society, so their livelihood wouldn't be dependent on one or two people's financial health.

You may say that these things will never happen, and that therefore it's pointless to discuss them. But my point here is to argue that the family structure is not an absolute necessity, as it's been represented to us.

The supposed necessity of the family structure

Any institution that is as fundamental to our societies as the family structure will, whenever possible, be portrayed as necessary and be defended as strongly as possible. The strongest possible kind of argument in support of a social system, as I've already discussed, is biological necessity. Therefore it should be no surprise that the family structure is defended in those terms.

We are told that the human species, homo sapiens, has as part of its genome the instincts needed to form male-female pairings which take exclusive care of their young. But this is contrary to all anthropological knowledge. Many societies today still operate under the system of extended families or even communal child raising. In some societies, children are raised by their mothers, and her male sexual partners only provide resources. In some societies, polygamist families also have existed or still exist.

So this belief that the family structure is biologically necessary is just nonsense. Just because it is the dominant child rearing institution in Western societies does not make it part of human biology, unless you're so bigoted that you believe Western people represent all of humanity (not to mention the entire history of humanity).

But we can take the argument even further and say that even planned communities and experiments like the kibbutzim and Summerhill School should be impossible if the family structure was a biological necessity. Think of what that means. Eating is a biological necessity. Sleeping is a biological necessity. Without doing those things, we eventually die. We can't contrive ways to live for years without eating or sleeping, no matter how hard we try. Any "non-eating" community would die off pretty quickly (unless they're cheating by eating when no one's looking, like the breatharians do). So how could communities which raise children differently even survive?

One may reply that the family structure may not be an absolute biological necessity, but rather a preferable, or traditional, structure for child rearing. But once we concede that it is not necessary, we enter the murkier realm of ethics. It is pointless to question that which is necessary: we do not debate whether it is good or bad for humans to eat or sleep, only how these needs are fulfilled, because they must be fulfilled. But if the family structure is not necessary, then we can question its existence as an institution, which entails answering Noam Chomsky's question: can we give a justification for the existence of the family structure, if we take into account the interests of everyone involved?

As I've stated previously, we can justify certain actions which are undertaken within the family structure, most notably those aiming at the well-being and security of children, but these actions could be undertaken under many other child rearing structures. So the question becomes, can the family structure itself be justified?

It certainly has the power of tradition behind it, as well as that of social acceptability. But there are other important ethical principles than tradition and social acceptability: the duty to not inflict unnecessary harm, human rights, the necessity of consent, reciprocity, all of which are broken by the family structure in a massive and unjustifiable way.

The family structure is not set up to fend off harm to children. That is part of what it does, but it's not what it's set up for. We can tell what any institution actually is for, its actual purpose, by looking at its history, how it works, where the power goes and where the money goes, and its concrete results. If you do all this, I think that you can come up with a pretty good argument that the actual purposes of the family structure are the perpetuation of class inequality and the imposition of conformity on children (two purposes which are also part of the schooling system, on which I will talk in a bit).

There is, then, a fundamental contradiction between the belief that children should not be abused and the supposed right to a family, as supported by the United Nations. Belief in such a right, especially when backed by reputable human rights organizations, reinforces the fallacious equation between the family structure and children's well-being.

One may counter with some romanticism about the love that parents have for their children, that the parent-child relationship serves the purpose of love and care. I want to make this point again because I think it's of prime importance: love and care may be a part of family structures around the world, but that's not what they're for. A child rearing structure built around providing love and care for children would not have an inbuilt near-total inequality between children and their caretakers.

Some may try to argue in favor of the family structure in other ways. For example, people often set up a false dichotomy between pedagogy and neglect, implying that child rearing must be either controlling and strict, or lax and neglectful, and that "bad parents" most often employ the latter. But this is a false dichotomy, because neglectful parents are still exerting their control over the child by withdrawing needed resources from them. They are still engaged in the process of pedagogy. As Alice

Miller points out in For Your Own Good:

> But an honest rejection of all forms of manipulation and of the idea of setting goals does not mean that one simply leaves children to their own devices. For children need a large measure of emotional and physical support from the adult. This support must include the following elements if they are to develop their full potential:
>
> 1. Respect for the child
> 2. Respect for his rights
> 3. Tolerance for his feelings
> 4. Willingness to learn from his behavior

The fact that parents can be either strict or neglectful does not prove that one of those alternatives must be valid and the other invalid (strict=good, neglectful=bad). Both alternatives are invalid because neither takes children's developmental needs into account.

The question may arise: what about "bad children"? Can't children be bad too, and doesn't that mean they need to be controlled? Of course there are children who bully other children, for instance, because they are being bullied by their own parents. People who are victimized will usually seek to take it out on those equal or lower on the totem pole (hence the bromide that the frustrated worker takes it out on his wife, who takes it out on the children, who take it out on the pets). It's easier for children to strike against other children instead of striking against adults.

What should we do in such situations? It seems to me that the very worse thing to do in such a situation would be to coerce the child into staying with the people who have been bullying it. But that's precisely the answer given to us by the advocates of parental control: that the control which has educated the child into becoming a bully should be used to stop the child from causing further damage. This is about as stupid as saying that shooting yourself in the foot should be remedied by more shots in the foot, because more gun shots will eventually heal your foot.

What we do know from adults is that behavioral problems, when they are actually problems and not just healthy traits that other people want to suppress, are not lowered or eliminated by attempting to exert more authoritarian control on the people with the problem. Putting people in jails and prisons does not lower crime rates (otherwise the United States, which has the highest proportion of its citizens in jail of any country in the world, would be a safe haven). Surveillance technologies do not make people more moral, and neither do strict religious hierarchies.

What does happen, however, is that authoritarian families make the exercise of control more familiar to children. Children who are raised to believe that authoritarianism is acceptable in family relationships grow up into adults who believe that authoritarianism is acceptable in society. The screaming, scheming, privacy-busting parents are a police state in miniature. The father who uses corporal punishment and verbal tactics on his children is a small version of a dictatorship. The mother who imposes religious beliefs (or any other kind of beliefs) under the threat of being deprived of love or support is a friendly neighborhood theocracy.

Is it any wonder that traditionally monarchs were called the fathers of the nation and were associated with divine power? That the men who endorsed the U.S. Constitution are referred to as "Founding Fathers"? That we talk about the "fatherland" and the "motherland"? The power elite has always sought to cultivate a psychology of complete obedience to power, and have supported the family structure as the best way to mold people's psychologies around a similar form of complete obedience, that between the parents (traditionally, the father) and the child.

The childist omerta

The term "omerta" is used to talk about a certain code of conduct used by the Mafia around the world: a "code of silence" by which members of the Mafia are forbidden from speaking to the authorities about their fellow members' activities. The entire organization operates under the principle that staying quiet, and giving advantages to those who stay quiet under legal pressure, is the best way to keep their organization from being dismantled.

A family is, in some respects, a small Mafia. Parents sometimes commit illegal activities (such as corporal punishment or child abuse), which they don't want to become known. Most parents use unethical control against their children, sometimes in ways they would not want to become known.

Let's start with some extreme, and famous, examples. In 2008, it was revealed that a known rapist named Josef Fritzl held his daughter captive for 24 years in his cellar, with seven children being the result of her rape at his hands. According to her testimony, he started to rape her when she was 11. In South Lake Tahoe, California, Jaycee Lee Dugard was kidnapped at the age of 11, raped by her abductor (who was another known rapist), gave birth to two children, and kept in a tent in the backyard until she was rescued at 29.

Everyone is aghast at these events and says, "how is such a thing possible?" There are many ways to analyze this question. We can talk about the psychology involved. We can talk about how both of the tormentors had previous convictions for rape. We can talk about the complicity, or lack thereof, of the wives of the tormentors. But one question that particularly preoccupies us here is: how did they remain hidden for so long?

Perhaps we can get a hint of this by looking at a quote from one of the people who lived next to Jaycee Lee Dugard's prison:

> I asked my husband, 'Why is he living in tents?' she said. And he said, 'Maybe that is how they like to live.'

That's a very interesting statement because it tells us that silence was the principle followed here. Yes, perhaps they simply like to live in tents while having an entire house also available. But there are much somber possibilities as well. The idea that perhaps these possibilities should be investigated did not occur to them, because of the parenting conspiracy of silence.

This omerta, as I refer to it, is comprised of three parts:

1. The inviolability of the home ("a man's home is his castle"/"they have a right to their privacy").

2. The inferiority of children ("he/she must have done something wrong"/"children must obey their parents"/"children need discipline in order to be moral").

3. The agreed-upon ownership of the rights of children ("we can't intervene in family decisions"/"it's their child, they can do whatever they want"/"my house my rules").

These three parts, put together, create the omerta. It's hard to even be aware of abuse when we believe in the inviolability of the home. It's hard to be on the side of the child when we're trained to believe that they deserve it. And it's hard to want to report abuse when we believe that parents are basically allowed to do whatever they want. This deadly combination creates the conditions of sustained child abuse, all the way down the line from your run-of-the-mill verbal and physical abuse to the extreme cases I've given.

The perceived necessity of the modern family structure provides the ideological underpinning that gives credibility to these three parts. Another ideological underpinning is the right to privacy. We imagine the family and the family home as a bubble of ownership, within which we have no right to pry. In our highly individualistic countries, we believe that the right to privacy is of prime importance, and tend to label anything that goes against it as dictatorial.

The end result is, as we know, a system where abuse (legal and illegal) is widespread. And this omerta is also internalized by children over time. I know that as a child there were a lot of things I didn't tell my parents or other adults, and I've found this to be true of other people as well. I've read of many cases where the child never talked to its parents about sexual abuse taking place outside the home. As a child, you assimilate the principle of secrecy from your own parents and it becomes part of your life. Many people report that they didn't want to affect their parents with bad news. Where do you think they got that idea?

The omerta extends to how parents talk to other

parents. There is a definite party line that must be followed: new parents always talk about how happy and fulfilled they are, even when they are suffering or live in despair. I will quote stories from such parents in the next chapter. For now, I will say that the omerta provides powerful support for procreation: prospective breeders only hear how rewarding and fulfilling it is to have children, and they have no particular reason to believe otherwise.

I don't think anyone is so deluded as to believe that having a baby is no work whatsoever, but the negatives of having children are either omitted or portrayed as irrelevant compared to the positives. And everyone knows how new parents are insufferable in talking constantly about their children. In doing so, they provide a propaganda front for procreation, and ultimately for natalism and its objectification of women and children.

The omerta also benefits childism, in that it represses awareness of child abuse. The first thing bigots will try to do is to portray their victims as not being victims at all, but rather persecutors, and silencing abuse is one good way to do that. If the abuse is not known, then any attempt to get rid of prejudice will be met with disbelief. What's the point of arguing against childism if we believe children are being treated benevolently?

You may know the famous story of Sigmund Freud. Early in his career, he uncovered the depth of abuse and depravity that children were exposed to, but his findings were ill-received. Realizing that he could never have a career if he told the truth, he decided to bury this awareness under such things as the "Oedipus Complex" and the "Electra Complex," blaming children's drives for their own abuse. This has led to a century of ignorance about children's experiences. As Alice Miller explains in For Your Own Good:

> Freud shrank from the reality that was being revealed to him, from that time on allying himself instead with the patriarchal society of which he was a member (especially once he was over forty and, as a family man, had become a respected authority figure). He founded the psychoanalytic school, which likes to think of itself as revolutionary but in fact remains committed to the old ideas of casting blame on the helpless child and defending the powerful parents. When a patient who has been sexually abused as a child enters analysis, she will be told that it is her fantasies and desires that she is relating, because in reality she dreamed as a child of seducing her own father.

It's hard to exaggerate the effect that psychoanalysis, as the accepted "scientific" psychiatric position, has had in perpetuating childism.

The importance of schooling

While I've concentrated on the family structure as

the main vehicle of childism, schooling cannot be forgotten as another major way in which children are oppressed.

Within the childist worldview, schools serve the main role of being sources of "success." Children will become "successful" adults if they go to the best schools and receive the right diplomas. It is of prime importance to most parents that their children fit as well as possible into the schooling system. All children are taught to strive for a good college education in order to be able to compete for the best jobs.

The real purpose of schooling, as we know it, is not to educate children and develop their intellect. We know this because, as I pointed out before, we can tell the purpose of an institution by looking at how it's structured. And in the case of schooling, we know it is set up along the following lines:

1. The constant, unrelenting use of testing as the sole measure of success.
2. Competitive or independent learning.
3. Authoritarian class structure (teacher-student).
4. Strong disrespect of students' rights (right of free speech, freedom of movement, freedom of dress, amongst others).
5. A generally fixed curriculum.
6. Choice of textbooks made by bureaucrats.
7. At least in the United States, different strata of school quality depending on their location (poor, predominantly black neighborhoods get a worse education than rich, white neighborhoods).

The first two are especially crucial, but all seven points add up to this: that schooling is clearly designed as a tool of indoctrination, not as a tool of learning. And we know this is the truth because, in this case, we know how the institution came about: this authoritarian and elitist model was copied from the Prussian educational model created in the early 19th century (which followed most of the points listed above), and was adopted gradually by other Western countries during the 19th century. While its original function was to educate the military class, its role expanded to creating a docile work force, and has been inextricably linked with the rise of corporate capitalism. As Alfie Kohn writes in No Contest:

> [I]t may well be that genuine education, which is decidedly not the consequence of our schooling, may not even be its chief purpose. The point of competition, suggests education critic George Leonard, is 'not really to help students learn other subjects, but to teach competition itself.' David Campbell similarly observes that 'the whole frantic, irrational scramble to beat others is essential for the kind of institution our schools are... [namely,] bargain-basement personnel screening agencies for business and government... Winning and losing are what our schools are all about, not education.' Just as standardized testing chiefly prepares one to be a competent taker of standardized tests, so competition

perpetuates itself- and often does so to the exclusion of the subject supposedly being taught.

This is why I said earlier that schooling shares with the family structure two main purposes: the perpetuation of class inequality and the imposition of conformity. The fact that poor people do not have access to an equal quality of schooling, that they are constantly evaluated and sorted in a way that gives more advantage to those who had better schooling, and that only the richest amongst us have the opportunity to attend the most prestigious colleges, creates an elitist system which fixes economic and social class. The fact that students compete with each other, the authoritarian class structure, the disrespect for students' rights, and the near total absence of choice within the curriculum, create an obedient adult.

This last statement may seem strange to some, since competition has been lauded as the key to freedom. Belief in competition is particularly prevalent in the United States (which may help explain how it scores so low compared to others), but it is part of all Western schooling systems. But competition has nothing to do with a good education, or a good performance in any field. Children who are forced to compete with each other show less capacity to learn, lower motivation, higher distrust of others, and lower creativity.

The book No Contest, by Alfie Kohn, discusses the sociological data accumulated about the effects of cooperation and competition in various settings, most notably classrooms. The results there are startling and nearly unanimous: competition does not work, and competitive schooling hinders children's learning and development. Hundreds of studies show that cooperation is almost always the best way for children to learn. Kohn identifies four main reasons:

> First, competition often makes kids anxious and that interferes with concentration. Second, competition doesn't permit them to share their talents and resources as cooperation does, so they can't learn from one another. Finally, trying to be Number One distracts them from what they're supposed to be learning. It may seem paradoxical, but when a student concentrates on the reward (an A or a gold star or a trophy), she becomes less interested in what she's doing. The result: Performance declines.

Equally importantly, competition fosters conformity and obedience to the rules. After all, a competition forces all participants to follow its rules in order to win. It is a waste of time for a child to, for example, develop a deeper interest in a topic of study, when such interest is not conducive to success in testing. Unlike children in Summerhill School, children in regular schools must always study to the tests, not to what interests them, because anything beyond that is effort wasted.

Children are naturally cooperative, but having to go through more than twelve years of constant testing and competition in all areas hardens their heart. To most adults, cooperation in any field is trivial, childish, unworthy of serious consideration (even I wasn't against competition until I read Kohn's book). Serious and important schools, workplaces, sports, political systems, lifestyles, and even games, are competitive ones.

Some propose homeschooling as the solution to the evils of public schooling. But homeschooling still inscribes itself within the context of the family structure, and therefore provides no solution at all to the purposes which are shared by both schooling and the family structure. If it is true that most parents are not qualified to raise children, then it is equally true that most parents are not qualified to be teachers.

While it is true that homeschooled children generally get better test results, this does not necessarily mean that they are better educated. It only means that they are better at taking tests. While the added freedom given to children compared to the regimentation of school may be helpful to them, they do not gain any ability to cooperate with others (unless they do so with their siblings) or to learn how to be ethical (as children learn ethics only through self-governance).

The importance of schooling to natalism is fairly straightforward. Natalism posits that children must exist to fulfill some social or economic duty (such as consuming, growing the GDP, financing other people's retirements, filling highly skilled jobs, or driving innovation). Schooling is the main way that children are trained to fulfill these duties, along with the mass media and economic institutions. At the same time, those children who successfully go through the schooling system are rewarded by better, higher paying jobs, which reinforces their belief in the system and gives hope to the next generation (although economic downturns do cut the connection between education and rewards to some extent, which makes people feel a sense of injustice).

Ultimately, schooling is an exercise in self-fulfilling prophecies. We believe that children must be molded in an authoritarian hierarchy, some children become "successful" by going through this hierarchy, therefore we conclude that the belief was true all along. We hold to certain stereotypes about the educational abilities and personalities of girls and children of color, teachers subconsciously treat them differently based on stereotypes, and thus the belief is proven[14]. Some companies are even propagating the sexist position that "boys and girls learn differently" (on the basis of pseudo-science) in order to sell books, gendered tutoring services, teacher and parent training, and even bogus school certifications. And the more we treat gender differently, the more the prophecy will fulfill itself.

The order/value gap

I have previous mentioned the existence of an order/value gap, in the context of childists demanding that children internalize parental orders. I've pointed out that one can only believe internalization is necessary and valid if one already believes that parental orders must be followed by the child without question.

I call my argument the order/value gap because it proposes the existence of an unbridgeable gap between orders given to an individual and the individual's values[15]. This is not an issue of morality (i.e. "you should not follow orders") but an issue of logic: person A giving an order to person B, no matter who person A and B are in relation to each other (even if person A is God itself!), cannot in any way entail that person B has an obligation to obey.

This may seem like a technical point, but it has profound consequences on the issue of childism. If true, it shows that parental orders cannot, logically, entail moral obligations on the part of the child. This also includes orders of the sort "I am your parent, I gave birth to you, therefore you should do X"; no matter their reason or source, no order can entail moral obligation. This is not to say that a person cannot personally feel obligated to do something on the basis of an order (e.g. because they are threatened with violence or loss of status if they disobey), but this is the result of their own values, not a necessary result of the order itself.

I must first define two terms:

An *intersubjective proposition* is a proposition about things which are not accessible to all observers, but which are rather the result of group adherence or belief. For example, the proposition "God has a son who died for our sins" is self-evident to a Christian believer, but is nonsensical to anyone who does not already share their conception of "God." It is therefore an intersubjective proposition in the sense that I've defined.

An *objective proposition* is a proposition about things which are accessible to everyone (at least in theory), things which do not depend on any specific group adherence or belief. For example, the proposition "the universe is approximately 13.8 billion years" is theoretically accessible to everyone, and can be evaluated, measured, and corrected by anyone with the scientific knowledge to do so. Anyone, no matter their beliefs, can understand (and decide if they agree or disagree with) the concept of "age of the universe" and "13.8 billion years." Is it therefore an objective proposition in the sense that I've defined.

Based on these definitions, the argument is simple: no amount of intersubjective propositions can justify an objective proposition because, no matter how many such proposition you chain up, they will always remain dependent upon the group beliefs. Only objective propositions can justify other objective propositions.

Let me give you a fictional example to illustrate this, with C being a Christian and A being an atheist:

C: "God says that homosexuals are sinful."
A: "Okay."
C: "That's why you must never commit any homosexual acts."
A: "Hang on. First, you said God says it. I am not going to dispute that: you're the Christian, you would know. But now you're saying that I have to follow this rule. Why?"
C: "Because whatever God says is what you should do. God is the ultimate standard of morality."
A: "You are welcome to believe whatever you want about God, but I don't believe in God, so I am not really bothered by any of this. What you think God says has no relevance to me."
C: "But God is real, and he will send you to Hell if you disobey him!"
A: "So, might makes right then. That's ultimately what these things always reduce to, isn't it? Once again, I understand that you believe that God is real, and that you believe in Hell, but you haven't proven anything to me. Unless you can prove to me that God is real and how I can verify the validity of God's commands, all you have to give me is a threat of force. I might be scared by a threat of force if it was real, but acting out of being scared does not mean I accept any obligation as being valid."

The initial intersubjective statement in this example is "God says that homosexuals are sinful" (by the way, the opposite, "God says that homosexuals are not sinful," would also be an intersubjective statement), and all subsequent statements are elaborations on it. Because the initial statement is tied to Christianity as a belief system, the entire argument is tied to Christianity as a belief system. The only way for the Christian to break the loop would be to propose some objective statement which vouches for those other statements (which is what Christian apologetics is for, although it has failed miserably in all cases).

This argument applies to any attempt to impose moral obligation from some standpoint external to the individual, be it religion, politics, or prejudices when they imply some moral obligation. Childism, for example, entails that a parent's order conveys a moral obligation to the child. So we can construct a dialogue similar to the previous, with P being a parent and C being a perspicacious child who studies ethics:

P: "I want you to clean your room."
C: "Why?"
P: "Because I am your father and I order you to clean your room."
C: "I accept that you are my father, but your desire that I clean my room is a personal desire of yours which does not provide justification for me having an obligation to clean my room."
P: "You are obliged to do it because you should always obey your parents."
C: "As a parent, you believe that children should always obey their parents. But I see no particular reason to believe that to be true. To do so, I would have to accept that children are inferior to their parents, which is not self-evident to me at all."

P: "Fine. You are obliged to do it because I'll take away your computer and phone if you refuse."
C: "Ah. now we see the violence inherent in the system!"

Okay, so the child in my example is a fan of Monty Python. My point is that the same argument applies: the proposition "I want you to clean your room" is a (subjective) desire, and it is predicated on the proposition "you should always obey your parents," which is inter-subjective, as it depends on belief in childism. If one believes in childism, then all orders are justified. If one does not believe in childism, then no orders are justified.

You may think that this is far too black and white, and that surely some orders are justified, that there's nothing outlandish about asking a child to clean its room. Certainly I don't deny that it can be perfectly justified for a child to clean its room, but the justification does not, and cannot, come from any order.

So where do moral obligations come from? They can come from any source which is not an institution or hierarchy trying to impose them externally. We get our moral obligations mainly from our own beliefs about morality. We usually feel morally obligated to protect our most cherished values, and to destroy that which we value the least.

For example, we might feel a moral obligation to tell the truth in certain circumstances, such as when we observe a despicable action which goes otherwise unreported. Some people will go to extraordinary lengths to become "whistleblowers" in various situations. Others, who value their friendships dearly, may feel a moral obligation to help their friends in times of need.

The name of the order/value gap is meant to follow the template of the famous is/ought gap, which proposes an unbridgeable gap between statements of fact and statements of morality[15]. The is/ought gap disproves many positions about meta-morality[16], including the concept of "evolutionary mandate" discussed in chapter 1, as well as natalist arguments. Natalist arguments are based on political facts, and from these facts we are supposed to derive some obligation to have more children, but it's impossible to derive moral statements from factual statements.

This has far-reaching consequences for procreative ethics. Self-professed experts claim to know the correct reproductive policies to adopt on the basis of some economic or social issue, but these statements of fact cannot alone translate into some moral obligation on the part of women to have children. Any argument for natalism which involves external facts necessarily cannot prove that we should procreate.

The upshot is that the decision to procreate cannot be justified by abstract considerations, and can only be justified by introducing the other two sides of the triangle, the interests of women and children, making discussions of childism, antinatalism, feminism and abortion all the more important.

Childism and Christianity

In the West, the Christian religion has dominated discussions about procreation and the role of children. Catholics still uphold the Biblical imperative to "be fruitful and multiply," although many disagree with this verse. The Bible also sets rules regarding parents' dominion over children, instructing children to obey their parents, parents to violently punish their children, and prescribing the execution of children for specific forms of disobedience.

And then there is the story of Abraham and Isaac in Genesis 22, which is perhaps the most emblematic of the religious attitude towards children. God orders Abraham to sacrifice his only son Isaac as a burnt offering to him. So Abraham brings his son Isaac to a mountain designated by God, puts him on an altar, and prepares to stab him to death. An angel appears at the last second, telling Abraham that he's passed the test and that he doesn't have to kill his son, letting him kill a ram instead.

In this story, Abraham's complete blind obedience is portrayed as a holy virtue. That is the fundamental lesson underlying God's cruelty and Abraham's willingness to kill his child: that these things are not born out of evil but out of good, because obedience is good and superiors (whether they be gods or parents) may do whatever they want.

Alice Miller discusses this story extensively in her book The Untouched Key. I think her discussion of the paintings made of the story is particularly relevant:

> In none of the paintings can we detect any questioning in Isaac's eyes, questions such as "Father, why do you want to kill me, why is my life worth nothing to you? Why won't you look at me, why won't you explain what is happening? How can you do this to me? I love you, I trusted in you. Why won't you speak to me? What crime have I committed? What have I done to deserve this?"
>
> Such questions can't even be formulated in Isaac's mind. They can be asked only by someone who feels himself on equal footing with the person being questioned, only if a dialogue is possible, only if one can look the other in the eye. How can a person lying on a sacrificial altar with hands bound, about to be slaughtered, ask questions when his father's hand keeps him from seeing or speaking and hinders his breathing? Such a person has been turned into an *object*. He has been dehumanized by being made a sacrifice; he no longer has a right to ask questions and will scarcely even be able to articulate them to himself, for there is no room in him for anything besides fear.

But perhaps the most telling statement about children in the Bible is that uttered by Paul in I Corinthians. In Childism, Elisabeth Young-Bruehl discusses the implications of this statement:

> "When I was a child, I spake as a child, I understood as a child, I thought as a child," Paul of Tarsus told the Corinthians (I Cor. 13:11), self-righteously invoking his own uplifting conversion to Christianity. "When I became a man, I put away childish things." The essence of Christian childism is this rejection of children as sinfully childish. Adoration of a sinless, holy child, Jesus, who is superior to all adults and who will rule over all children ("Suffer the little children to come unto me") is a rejection of disrespectful children. Jesus was never a human child, never fallible or imperfect like all other human children, who, in some later Christian theological treatises, were presented as originally sinful- that is, born sinful.

In Christianity, as in childism in general, the child is seen as a duality: the substance of childhood is that of amorality and triviality, but "good" children, in this case Jesus, are innocent and pure. The unsaved are directly liked with childishness: they are also amoral, trivial, not concerned with the higher things of the Spirit, and therefore sinful, not of God.

The Christian hatred and disgust of children has consequences for children in the real world: it obviously justifies the imposition of religious indoctrination on children, but it also justifies circumcision, the rigid enforcement of gender roles, the repression of sexual impulses, and the rejection of homosexual children, amongst other injustices. All these things are related to each other: Christianity, like all authoritarian religions, prescribe that each person has a specific place in the social order, and that anyone who refuses to take their proper place will be corrected.

What it means for women is that women should shut up, get married to a man, have children, and worship the Lord. And there are still women who follow this blueprint, although fortunately the vast majority of people have abandoned it. But they have not, for the most part, abandoned the idea of having children.

Conclusion

Since the study of childism is still very new, I have no doubt that most people would deny its existence (just as most people two thousand years ago would deny that there was any problem with slavery, except the slaves). However, the position that childism exists and is a huge worldwide problem does explain the current overwhelming consensus about the way to treat children and their place in society. Like most prejudices, childism is considerably weaker than it was centuries ago[17], but this is more of a statement of how horribly difficult life was in the past for anyone who didn't have privilege than about the present. The fact that children in the West are no longer uniformly "disciplined" through furious beatings and constant fear, and are no longer treated like work slaves, is a consolation, but it does not erase the existence of childism nevertheless, or the existence of violence against children not only in the West but around the world.

I hope I have made my point in this chapter that much of the support for procreation and natalism is supported by childist prejudice, all the way from the ideological rationalizations for childism to the schooling system. Not only that, but the existence of childism makes children's lives much harder than they have to be, the same children whose existence was pushed by our current procreative ethics.

In the next chapters, I am going to change the subject and examine another ideological position, antinatalism.

Chapter 5
Antinatalism

What is antinatalism?

Antinatalism, generally speaking, is the position that procreation is wrong.

While antinatalism as a distinct idea and a movement is a very new phenomenon, its ideas are not new. Many pessimist thinkers throughout history have taken such a stance. We can go all the way back to the eleventh century, when secular Arab poet Abul ʿAla Al-Maʿarri wrote the following in a collection called Luzūm mā lam yalzam (which can be read in Studies in Islamic Poetry by Reynold Alleyne Nicholson):

> If ye unto your sons would prove
> By act how dearly them ye love
> Then every voice of wisdom joins
> To bid you leave them in your loins

He also wrote to "refrain from procreation, for its consequence is death." He seems to have followed this advice, as he reportedly wanted his headstone to say:

> My sire brought this on me, but I on none.

One notable pessimist thinker who adopted antinatalist ideas was German philosopher Arthur

Schopenhauer. He wrote his most famous antinatalist lines in the essay On the Sufferings of the World:

> Again, you may look upon life as an unprofitable episode, disturbing the blessed calm of non-existence. And, in any case, even though things have gone with you tolerably well, the longer you live the more clearly you will feel that, on the whole, life is a disappointment, nay, a cheat...
>
> If children were brought into the world by an act of pure reason alone, would the human race continue to exist? Would not a man rather have so much sympathy with the coming generation as to spare it the burden of existence? or at any rate not take it upon himself to impose that burden upon it in cold blood.

For more on antinatalist ideas before the recent developments which I will now discuss, I recommend the book The Conspiracy Against the Human Race, by Thomas Ligotti, as an excellent overview.

There are two books in particular that have helped to codify antinatalism as a distinct ideology and in establishing its main arguments. The first is L'Art de Guillotiner les Procréateurs (which I quoted earlier on the subject of the objectification of children in natalism), by Belgian activist and poet Théophile de Giraud, released in 2006. In it, de

Giraud systematically goes through the rationalizations for procreation, the real reasons why people procreate, and lays down a number of antinatalist arguments.

The second foundational book of the antinatalist ideology is Better Never to Have Been, by South African philosopher David Benatar, also released in 2006. Benatar's book not only discusses the arguments which we now know as standard, but he also discusses the relevance of antinatalism to reproductive rights, artificial reproduction, abortion, the population question, human extinction, and suicide.

Ever since then, other books have been written on antinatalism[18], but these two particular books are most relevant to our topic. Antinatalism has a direct bearing on the procreation question: if it is morally wrong to procreate, then the pro-natalism side has a huge burden of proof to shed, that of demonstrating that we should still procreate despite it being morally wrong.

That is not to say that procreation being generally wrong would settle the issue once and for all. We do allow things that are generally wrong in specific cases where they can do more good than bad: I've pointed out before that some coercive actions (such as firefighters breaking down doors or windows, or pulling someone out of the way of a moving car) can be justified on a pragmatic basis, to bring about some obvious, undisputed good (such as fighting fires or preventing car accidents). Benatar, for example, does acknowledge that there are some limited situations where procreation may bring about such obvious, undisputed good, although the situations he discusses have to do with drastic underpopulation and have nothing to do with the world we live in.

Antinatalism being true does, however, completely change the nature of the conversation. It is usually argued that procreation is an obvious, undisputed good, and all anyone argues about is the balance required between population growth and environmental or social concerns. But antinatalism, if true, entails that procreation is, generally speaking, wrong. It clashes head-on with the current frameworks.

But before we address the issue of procreation from an antinatalist perspective, we must first look at what antinatalism is about and what antinatalist arguments there are. So let me first quote de Giraud:

> Answer without flinching: if there existed a solution that could abolish the totality of all evils inflicted on disastrous humanity, if it was possible, by some simple remedy, incredibly cheap, immediately accessible, scrupulously inoffensive, of absolute and definitive efficiency, to stop all distress, all cries, all cries of pain, all pathologies, all protests of ill-being, all despair, all cataclysms, all anxiety, all unhappiness, in short all tortures afflicting the human species, would you have the macabre

171

> stupidity to reject such a remedy, to disdain such a miracle cure? No, that goes without saying.
>
> Well this solution does exist, and the mysterious is thereby delivered to us: it consists simply, in its saintly simplicity, to not procreate...

And David Benatar:

> [O]ne implication of the view that coming into existence is always a serious harm is that we should not have children. Some anti-natalist positions are founded on either a dislike of children or on the interests of adults who have greater freedom and resources if they do not have and rear children. My anti-natalist view is different. It arises, not from a dislike of children, but instead from a concern to avoid the suffering of potential children and the adults they would become...

Benatar raises a point which merits some attention, the issue of childfreedom as opposed to antinatalism. It's important to make that distinction, because there are many people who are childfree and not antinatalists, and there are antinatalists who are not childfree.

Childfree people are defined as people who do not have children and do not intend to have children. It is, therefore, not a moral position but a statement of fact and intention. An individual may be childfree because they value their freedom and resources, because they don't feel like they could cope with having children, or because they dislike children, or for any other reason. There are as many reasons to be childfree as there are childfree people. Most childfree people do not believe that procreation is wrong as such, or that procreation is wrong in our current state of the world, but all do believe that procreation is the wrong thing to do for themselves and their own lives.

Antinatalists are defined by their ethical belief about procreation. Almost all antinatalists became antinatalists as adults, and some of them had children before they became antinatalists. There is nothing particularly weird about people regretting their past actions in the light of newfound beliefs, and it would be a rather odd person who didn't regret anything they ever did.

Adopting the antinatalist position may have all sorts of causes. Some people are attracted to antinatalism because they have a pessimistic view of human existence. Others (such as myself) are attracted to antinatalism because they've come into contact with the arguments and judged them as sound. Yet others are attracted to antinatalism because of feminist, environmental, anti-childist, or generally egalitarian commitments. There is no particularly "good" or "bad" way to become an antinatalist.

I admit that there are some antinatalists who dislike children, and there are some outright childist

173

antinatalists. Although some antinatalist arguments are concerned with children's welfare, and therefore contradict childism, there are other antinatalist arguments which are compatible with childism, so a childist antinatalist is not a contradiction. One can be a childist antinatalist, an anti-childist antinatalists, or anything in between. But it's impossible to be an anti-childist natalist.

There are many antinatalist arguments; for the sake of clarity, it is useful to divide them in categories. In his book, Benatar divides the arguments in two chapters: one devoted to the arguments which show that coming into existence is a harm, and one devoted to the arguments that life entails a wide variety of suffering, many of which happen to everyone.

The anonymous author of a blog called Why I'm Sold On Antinatalism (why-im-sold-on-antinatalism.blogspot.com/), no longer in operation, proposed a classification which I've found very useful. It consists of four different categories:

1. Ecological arguments. This is the sort of antinatalism promoted by the organization VHEMT (Voluntary Human Extinction MovemenT), probably the oldest antinatalist organization in the world. Arguments in this category pertain to the environmental destruction and animal suffering engendered by human existence. The most destructive thing you can do to the environment, far overshadowing any efforts on your part to help it, is to give birth to a new human being. Ecological

174

antinatalism simply takes this realization to its logical conclusion.

2. Philanthropic arguments. These arguments revolve around the prevention of suffering, or as Benatar puts it, that "coming into existence is a harm." Their common theme is that they specifically argue that being born is a bad thing for those who are born, unlike ecological or misanthropic arguments which usually argue that new human lives is a bad deal all around, which is why they are called "philanthropic."

3. Teleological arguments. The term "teleological" refers to the purpose or aim of something, and teleological arguments in theology aim to show that everything around us points to a design, and therefore some greater purpose. Teleological antinatalism, on the other hand, is about the absence of purpose served by procreation. If procreation is pointless, then why promote it, let alone actually do it?

4. Misanthropic arguments. These arguments are of the "life is a raw deal" sort. Not in the sense of simply whining about life, but to show that coming into existence entails a wide variety of serious harms which one should not be keen to expose new lives to.

These four categories of arguments are all part of the vast field of antinatalism, and simply represent different approaches to the proposition that procreation is wrong. They are all harmonious approaches, as well. Just to give one example, ecological arguments are relevant to misanthropic interests insofar as the devastation we inflict on the ecosystems we depend upon have a huge impact on the suffering we inflict on each other.

I do not mean to say that these four categories include all possible antinatalist arguments. For instance, I think one can make the case that feminist arguments deserve their own category as well, and I will get into those later on.

Like anti-childism, antinatalism is not a well-received position, and is equally belittled. Unlike anti-childism, it is highly unlikely that antinatalism ever will be a well-received position. But, given how uncritically the general public discuss natalist ideas, I think that antinatalism deserves a hearing. I happen to be an antinatalist and hope you will give its arguments a fair trial. Whether you agree with it or not in the end, antinatalism has a tremendous importance to the issue of procreative ethics. Even if antinatalist arguments are only partially right, they would entail quite a shift of perspective on the whole field. So I think it behooves all of us to examine them.

Untangling "life"

Many of the misunderstandings of antinatalist arguments come from equivocations of the word "life," therefore I need to clear these out before we get to the arguments proper.

Compare the following uses of the word "life":

1. Every life has ups and downs.
2. Life appeared on Earth around four billion years ago.
3. It's not worth it to bring disabled lives into this world.
4. My life is no longer worth living.

The first equivocation is covered by sentences 1 and 2. The word "life" in sentence 1 means the actual lifespan of individual human beings. We can say that my life has ups and downs, your life has ups and downs, and so on. The word "life" in sentence 2, on the other hand, does not refer to the lifespan of any organism (no organism is four billion years old), but rather to life as a form of organization of matter, or for short, the life-system. All individual lifespans ("life" as in 1) are part of the life-system ("life" as in 2), but the life-system is an abstract concept while lifespans are things experienced by organisms.

The second equivocation is covered by sentences 3 and 4. The word "lives" in sentence 3 means "lifespans not worth starting," since it refers to persons who are not yet born. The word "life" in sentence 4, on the other hand, refers to "a lifespan not worth continuing," since the person already exists.

These may seem like similar concepts, but they are actually quite different, and that difference is important. Apart from fanatical anti-abortion or irrational disability advocates, few people think that the standard for a life not worth starting is anywhere near that of lives worth continuing. As David Benatar points out:

> For instance, while most people think that living life without a limb does not make life so bad that it is worth ending, most (of the same) people also think that it is better not to bring into existence somebody who will lack a limb. We require stronger justification for ending a life than for not starting one.

As a more general expression of this difference, compare public acceptance of suicide and assisted suicide with public acceptance of contraception and abortion: while none of these are seen in a positive light, contraception and abortion are far more widely accepted than suicide and assisted suicide. In general, people ending their life is seen as much more outrageous than not starting a new life. There is definitely an asymmetry there.

The distinction is crucial to any discussion of procreative ethics, because procreative ethics is about how many lives should be started, not about how many lives should continue to exist; and yet so many people who think they are discussing procreative ethics fail to make the distinction at all, which is counterproductive.

But why is there a difference at all? The answer is simple: a person who already exists has values,

178

desires, attachments, goals, all things which make their life worth living for them. Lives not yet started do not have any of those things. Missing a limb does not nullify the values, desires, attachments and goals of the existing person who is missing the limb, but missing a limb does entail willfully starting a new life with a severe disadvantage for no clear reason.

People who defend the rights of the disabled will usually object to an argument like sentence 3 on the basis that disabled lives are worth living. But this misses the point completely. Obviously disabled lives are worth living and supporting, but this does not entail that they are worth starting. These are two completely different issues, with different moral principles underlying them.

Indeed, if antinatalism is true, then no life is worth starting, disabled or not. We just see it more easily in the case of starting a disabled life because we can intuitively see that forcing a new life to start with a severe disadvantage is profoundly unfair, regardless of our position on antinatalism.

Now let me go back to the equivocation of lifespans with the life-system. This equivocation lies at the core of one question frequently thrown in the face of antinatalists: "if you hate life so much, why don't you kill yourself?" Apart from being an extremely crass question, it shifts from one meaning to the other, as we can rephrase it like this:

"If you hate the life-system so much, why don't you

end your lifespan?"

Now we can see that there is no relation between the two parts of this question. As I said, my life, as well as that of most humans, is worth continuing because I have values, desires, attachments, goals, which make life worth living for me. At any rate, antinatalists do not hate the life-system, but they do look realistically at the effects of the existence of the life-system on this planet. It is not an emotional argument but a logical one.

The duty argument

The duty argument is perhaps the most accessible argument for antinatalism, because it relies on intuitions about justice that are upheld widely in all societies throughout history. All societies have upheld some form of the following:

1. We have a duty to not inflict suffering on others.

Restrictions against murder, assault, and theft are all obvious implementations of this principle. All societies have a strong abhorrence of inflicting unnecessary suffering, although they do disagree on what kinds of suffering are unnecessary. But it also includes all sorts of social mores like politeness and respect, which aim to grease the wheels of society and prevent friction between individuals.

On the other hand, the following is also widely held:

2. We do not have any duty to provide pleasure to others.

There are no laws stating that individuals have an obligation to provide pleasure to others. At worse, we think that people who are married have certain obligations towards each other (such as wives providing sex). Societies typically do allocate some resources for the provision of the needs of people who are unable to provide for themselves, but this has the aim of preventing further suffering, not to provide pleasure. We do not generally believe that we have an obligation to provide pleasurable experiences to others, such as a view of a sunset, ice cream, the laughter of a child, or anything like that. We see it as the individual's job to seek out pleasures in accordance with their preferences.

This brings us to the issue of asymmetries between pleasure and suffering: we do not, and cannot, evaluate pleasure and suffering on an equal footing because there are fundamental asymmetries between them. Pleasure and suffering are not just opposites of each other. And one of the ways in which they differ is in the issue of duties. We have a duty to not inflict suffering on others, but not a duty to provide pleasure.

For instance, we cannot "cancel out" a murder, an assault or a theft by giving some equivalent pleasure to the victim (or their family, in the case of murder). I can't hold off a assault conviction by playing them a song or baking them pies (or any number of songs

181

or pies). Even when pleasure is not concerned, we still don't think the infliction of suffering can always be canceled out. If a doctor saves your life and then, in a personal dispute later on, punches you in the face, we don't think that the punch was canceled out by the life-saving.

In Every Cradle is a Grave, Sarah Perry discusses an example where a person has to decide whether to administer a peanut or an ecstasy pill to a stranger, and what it tells us about the possibility of inflicting harm. The first interesting fact is that it's much more likely for that stranger to die of having been fed peanuts than ecstasy, and that therefore (if our guiding principle is to inflict the least harm) we should choose the ecstasy pill. But we can also draw larger conclusions:

> While many of us would certainly consider the pleasure of ecstasy in deciding whether to eat the pill or the peanut ourselves, it's proper and coherent not to consider the pleasurable effects of a potentially harmful action when it will be inflicted upon a non-consenting stranger whose values we do not know. This illustrates Seana Shriffrin's principal (sic) that, while it's morally acceptable to harm a stranger without his consent in order to prevent worse harm (e.g., to administer ecstasy in order to avoid administering a peanut or to break someone's arm in order to pull him from a burning car), it's not morally acceptable to harm a stranger without his consent in order

to provide a pure benefit. But the ecstasy example supports a stronger inference: when evaluating actions that will harm a non-consenting stranger, his potential pleasure doesn't count. When we're acting toward someone whose values we do not know, we should not think in terms of maximizing his utility, but in terms of minimizing our harm to him.

We can formulate the duty argument as follows:

1. We have a duty to not inflict suffering on others.
2. We do not have any duty to provide pleasure to others.
3. Lives include both pleasure and suffering.
4. Starting a new life implies providing pleasure and inflicting suffering to a new human life.
5. Therefore we have a duty not to start new lives.

The duty argument is in the category of philanthropic arguments, as it concerns the prevention of suffering which results from starting new lives.

As I've argued above, I believe that premises 1 and 2 are powerful intuitive propositions which are held universally true. Premise 3 is also an obvious statement: pretty much all human lives contain forms of pleasure and suffering which are common to all of us.

If any counter-argument can be made here, it is on the basis that procreation "does not count" towards points 1 and 2, that is to say, that procreation is exempt of the duty to not inflict suffering, or that it does fulfill some special duty to provide pleasure. This line of reasoning hinges upon the Non-Identity Problem, which I will discuss in the next chapter.

Misanthropic arguments

The basis for all misanthropic arguments is the wide variety of harms that human beings, and other sentient organisms, can experience. This is a mind-boggling task, to say the least, so I will content myself with generalities here.

We can roughly divide these harms in three categories: harms coming from the natural world, harms coming from society, and harms caused by new lives.

1. Nature is too harmful to bring new sentient life into it.

I already quoted Richard Dawkins' stark statement on the amount of suffering in nature from his book River Out of Eden. Suffice it to say that the natural world is not kind to sentience. The necessities built into our bodies, and the exquisite violence of nature, make a mockery of our desire to be free from pain. Most lifeforms depend on the death of other lifeforms in order to survive. Predation is everywhere and engenders an incalculable amount of suffering. Some viruses and bacteria inflict yet more suffering on top of that: crippling diseases, epidemics, plagues. The Black Plague alone (a tiny bacteria called Yersinia pestis) wiped out more than a third of Europe's population.

As for humans, the human body can come into this world with a great number of defects, going from the mundane to the fatal. And the same viruses and bacteria can give us a wide variety of diseases.

We are born with many biological needs: hunger (not just to eat anything, but to eat enough of a number of nutrients), thirst, to stay away from pain, to be shielded from the elements and extreme temperatures, to keep our organs in working order, and so on. We are also born with many psychological needs, many of which depend entirely on the goodwill of others. All these needs must constantly be satisfied, because failure to satisfy them brings us suffering.

The process of evolution which has guided the development of all life on this planet is a blind, stupid, thoughtless mechanism. While this may seem obvious, given that natural processes are not the product of design, it bears repeating because such considerations seem to disappear when we talk about putting new lives into this world. The natural order is inimical to sentience and it is wrong to bring new sentient life into it.

2. Human societies are too harmful to bring new people into them.

I don't think this needs much explanation. The

amount of war, genocide, executions, imprisonment, poverty and neglect perpetrated in the name of the nation or the government would give nature a run for its money. One must also include the lives ruined by pollution (currently reckoned to be the most important cause of death in the world), workplace negligence, land seizures, slavery, and servitude in the name of money. Then all the murders, assaults, rapes, frauds, and other mischief that individuals inflict on each other which, while being far lower in number than the previous two categories, still can make life a living Hell.

3. Humans inevitably inflict harm, therefore any new person will inevitably inflict harm on other sentient life.

Anyone who lives in a Western society will inflict suffering or benefit from someone else's suffering, no matter how hard they try to not do so.

A good example of that is that slavery is intertwined with Western imports, and any consumer of Western goods is living off of slave labor. This is a natural consequence of neo-liberalist predation, where organizations like the IMF and the World Bank leverage their money to devastate third-world welfare systems and services, or the US government overthrows worker-friendly governments, leaving Western corporations free to exploit desperate workforces.

Another important way in which we all benefit from

suffering is in our diet. Despite claims made by vegans, the sort of mass food system necessary to feed billions of people implies massive sentient death, even if you don't eat meat. Granted, our current meat-oriented food system does generate enormous amounts of wasteful suffering, but no one is entirely blameless.

As a very general rule, we can say that there is a certain quantity of suffering inherent to human life, and that Western capitalism and neo-liberalism seem to be particularly well developed ways of outsourcing misery and containing it. Low low prices for consumer goods depend on slave labor or servitude, and vastly underpaid workers at home. The demeaning part of sexual fulfillment is left to porn actresses, prostituted women, and women and girls in third-world countries. The demand for "law and order" is met by containing "criminality" and "disorder" within certain specific groups of people (drug users, black people and other "minorities," women) and destroying their lives.

I now turn to objections. First, there is an objection that applies more specifically to that last argument, and that is a sort of blasé dismissal based on how good one's life is, and simply going "oh, over there it's bad, but here it's not that bad!" The problem is that people who say this sort of thing benefit from the exploitation of slave labor, underpaid workers, and all the other people I mentioned in the previous paragraph. It's easy for privileged Western people to poo-poo the hardships their existence inflicts on other people, especially when those people are far away and different from them.

Where we're born, and to what family, is nothing more than a lottery; like all lotteries it is a sucker's bet, although some people still do win. This is hardly a reason for the lotto winners to ignore the fact that their monetary reward came from millions of other people paying for tickets with the same hopes that they did. I hope the analogy is obvious: people who are born in good circumstances shouldn't pretend that this is the case for everyone else too, or that their "victory" does not come at those people's expense.

Amongst the more general objections, perhaps the most common is of the style "suffering is a part of life so you should just deal with it." While this is true, it doesn't make much sense logically. Of course already existing people have to deal with it, but if suffering is a bad thing that we need to deal with, then why subject new human lives to it? The choice to subject them to it or not is precisely what is at issue: to procreate or not to procreate. To demand that we "deal with it" is therefore besides the point.

Now, none of these arguments in themselves provide the definite proof that procreation is wrong, although they all contribute to a more complete picture of what we're bringing new human lives into. Obviously the daily life of a random person on this planet is not as bad as, say, living in the middle of a genocide situation or a plague, situations in which we don't expect anyone to want children, but the stubborn refusal to confront the negatives of life contributes greatly to support for procreation.

There is one further objection that I need to clear out now, because it is very popular and recurs in many different situations, and that's the objection that life is not just about the negatives but is about the balance of pleasure and suffering. Usually this is accompanied by the statement that antinatalists are biased because they refuse to look at the positive side of being alive, and that procreation is acceptable because the average life has more pleasure than suffering.

There are many fundamental problems with this view. For one, it is based on the assumption that pleasure and suffering can be meaningfully measured and compared, but there is no known and proven method to do so. We can roughly measure the intensity of pleasure, or the intensity of suffering, experienced by one person, but we have no idea how the subjective experience of pleasure or suffering of one person compares with the subjective experience of pleasure or suffering of other people. In short, I know how I feel, and I know how you tell me you feel, but I have no way of comparing the two.

We can't even meaningfully compare different kinds of suffering, or different kinds of pleasure, within the same person. For example, physical pain is different from grief or depression, and yet they are all forms of suffering. Obviously we can make general statements: it is highly probable that any human being experiencing (for example) acute hunger for hours is experiencing more suffering than any human being experiencing a paper cut. But beyond such generalities, we can't make the kind of comparisons necessary to make statements about any "balance of pleasure and suffering," especially since we can't compare pleasure and suffering to begin with. Do eating your favourite meal and getting a leg cramp cancel out, or does one "weigh" more? Does winning a million dollars lottery weigh as much as losing a leg?

There is also the problem that not all forms of pleasure are said to make a life worth living, and not all forms of suffering are said to make a life not worth living. There are mundane examples of this: for instance, we think smoking is a bad habit, and have done much to reduce its popularity, even though it gives people pleasure.

A famous philosophical hypothetical, called the Experience Machine, asks us to imagine that we could plug ourselves to a machine that would permit us to experience any sort of life that we can imagine. This is pretty much the most efficient and personalized way to maximize pleasure that we could conceive, and yet most people say they wouldn't want to plug into the Experience Machine, and there are people who argue that the Experience Machine would lead humanity to extinction or something of the sort (not that an antinatalist would have anything against that).

So, does being plugged into the Experience

Machine make a life worth living? There is much doubt about that, even though the Experience Machine is the most extreme example of pleasure we can conceive. And if that sort of extreme example is dubious, then how can any pleasure be freed from the same doubt?

People who bring up this sort of objection talk about pleasures like looking at a sunset, eating ice cream, the laughter of a child, and other inoffensive things of that nature. All of that is nice and all, but does any of this stuff make a life worth living? Would we say a life that wasn't worth living now is worth living because it also happens to include one sunset or one ice cream scoop?

Another problem is that the quality of a life, as we measure it ourselves, does not merely depend on a simplistic criterion like the balance of pleasure and suffering. Benatar lists a lot of problem cases in chapter 3 of Better Never to Have Been. I will only quote one here, the most concrete, and therefore most easily understood, case:

> Arguably, once a life reaches a certain threshold of badness (considering both the amount and the distribution of its badness), no quantity of good can outweigh it, because no amount of good could be worth that badness. It is just this assessment that Donald ('Dax') Cowart made of his own life- or at least of that part of his life following a gas explosion that burnt two-thirds of his body. He refused extremely

painful, life-saving treatment, but the doctors ignored his wishes and treated him nonetheless. His life was saved, he achieved considerable success, and he reattained a satisfactory quality of life. Yet, he continued to maintain that these post-burn goods were not worth the costs of enduring the treatments to which he was subjected. No matter how much good followed his recovery, this could not outweigh, at least in his own assessment [the only assessment that matters], the bad of the burns and treatment that he experienced.

Even if we could somehow compare pleasure and suffering in any single life, simply canceling them out would not reflect the quality of that life.

Taking the pleasure and suffering contained in one person's life does not include the pleasure and suffering they caused in others. Most notably, since I am, after all, arguing against natalism, we must point to women's hardships in having a child, the parents' sacrifice of time and money, and society's sacrifice as a whole to sustain the children's well-being (including that of orphaned children and abused children).

Furthermore, we have no reason to believe that suffering and pleasure can "cancel out." We experience every suffering and every pleasure as a new event, and our life is going well or badly only insofar as we are experiencing suffering or pleasure at that moment. The idea that we can just add up every pleasure and substract every suffering has no connection with the way we live our lives. The way that pleasures and suffering events are distributed throughout our lives, and their intensity, also has a great impact on how we evaluate our life, regardless of how they "cancel out."[19]

There is also a more fundamental reason to reject the idea that pleasure and suffering "cancel out": suffering is primary, and pleasure exists in our organism mostly as a reaction to fulfilling a need and preventing more suffering. We experience pleasure when we eat good food because we are fulfilling our various needs for nutrition. If we do not eat, we starve. The pleasure and the suffering are both motivators to encourage the organism to avoid starving and keep the body fueled. It is the suffering that is the primary motivator: the pleasure only exists to reward us from keeping away from it.

This is not a new argument; Schopenhauer already pointed this out in his essay On the Sufferings of the World:

> I know of no greater absurdity than that propounded by most systems of philosophy in declaring evil to be negative in its character. Evil is just what is positive; it makes its own existence felt... It is the good which is negative; in other words, happiness and satisfaction always imply some desire fulfilled, some state of pain brought to an end.

I think that the idea of comparing pleasure and suffering in a mathematical way is a very modernist, Enlightenment sort of idea, based on the feeling people have that we should measure everything "scientifically" as an "objective" method of finding truth. But the simple fact is that we cannot measure everything "objectively." Suffering and pleasure are personal experiences which cannot be compared from person to person; the only point of reference we have about them are other, similar experiences.

It's also a concept that appeals to people who reject both antinatalism and unbridled natalism, or who like the idea that "the truth is somewhere between two extremes." It gives people wriggle room in an argument which otherwise provides none.

I've spent a lot of space debunking the balance objection because, as I said, it's a very common one. The problem is that natalists are solely concerned with the pleasures of life as an incentive for people to have children, so whenever someone brings up suffering as a counterpoint, they are accused of being "focused on suffering." Obviously all lives contain pleasure (except perhaps extremely short ones) and everyone is aware of that fact. But, as I've already discussed, there is a fundamental asymmetry between pleasure and suffering, as in the case of duties. Pleasures are not relevant to the issue of duties, because we have no duty to provide pleasure to others.

Arguments can be made on the basis of the

misanthropic evidence I've listed. Perhaps the most well-known one is the risk argument, which is usually formulated as a Russian Roulette analogy. Russian Roulette, in case you don't know, is a "game" where you put one bullet in a revolver, spin the cylinder and pull the trigger while aiming at your head (thereby giving 1 chance out of 6 that one will be shot). The revolver is then passed around the table until someone dies.

Suppose you're playing a game of Russian Roulette with other people. So far so good (although I'd severely question your judgment, but let's ignore that part). But now suppose a friend walks by and you try to convince him to join the game, unsuccessfully. So, frustrated at his refusal, you drag him to the table and strap him down, forcing him to take part in the game.

Regardless of their opinion about the dubious pastime of Russian Roulette, I think most people would say that this is clearly wrong. No one has the right to impose the risk of death or grievous bodily harm on someone else on a whim. If inflicting death or grievous bodily harm on someone in that situation is wrong, then putting them at risk of the same is also wrong. If the victim does end up dead or severely wounded, then the person who dragged them there would be held responsible legally and morally.

As the argument goes, this is an analogy for procreation. By starting a new life, we are also exposing it to a wide variety of harms, some of

195

which will affect that life and some which will not. While some harms may be more unlikely in certain geographical areas or in certain families, it's strictly impossible to bring about a new human life which will not be exposed to any harm at all, if only because the biological requirements of the human body themselves entail harms as well.

In this analogy, the victim of the forced Russian Roulette is the new lifespan being started, the person forcing them into the game represents the parents, the gun represents the life-system, and the bullets represent harms that will actually befall the victim's lifespan. If it is wrong to expose a person to the risk of harm through Russian Roulette, then it is equally wrong to expose a person to innumerable risks of harm through starting their lifespan.

The argument and analogy, I hope, are clear. In general, there is not much to say in objection apart from the perennial "deal with it." But in the book Debating Procreation, David Wasserman (who is arguing against David Benatar) tries to disprove the risk argument:

> Benatar's risk argument gains spurious strength, I suspect, from the Russian roulette simile he employs, which has prospective parents pointing a gun at the head of their future child; a gun with a high proportion of chambers loaded. This simile is misleading. As the literature on the ethics of risk imposition and distribution points out, it matters a great deal if the threatened harm

will be imposed intentionally. Shooting someone with a loaded gun is intentionally harming him, even if the discharge of the bullet had been far from certain. As David DeGrazia points out in discussing Shiffrin's harm argument, parents do not impose harm on their children so much as expose them to it, while making a concerted effort to avoid or mitigate it. And that is a far different matter for a non-consequentialist than imposing harm.

As a non-consequentialist, I have to completely disagree with Wasserman here. His objection is purely semantics and does not address the substance of the risk argument. To illustrate this, it will suffice to use his reframing and apply it to the Russian Roulette analogy:

> Suppose you're playing a game of Russian Roulette with other people. Now suppose a friend walks by and you try to convince him to join the game, unsuccessfully. So, frustrated at his refusal, you expose him to the risk of getting shot by dragging him to the table and forcing him to play, while making a concerted effort to mitigate it (by, for example, having a health kit nearby, or even a doctor).

Since the reframing does not change anything in our scenario (except the addition of some extra precautions), it does not refute the risk argument at all. Whether you formulate it as parents "imposing" harm or "exposing" children to harm, the end result is the same: children run a wide variety of risks of harm/suffering/death, and this is ultimately caused by their parents.

I think the point Wasserman is clumsily trying to make is that parents do not themselves perpetrate the harm that their children suffer. That is clearly false: most parents do perpetrate harm on their children, both physical and psychological. Parents do not, by far, perpetrate all the harm that befalls children, but the fact that they perpetrate at least some of it renders Wasserman's objection moot.

But beyond that, the objection does not take into consideration the fact that most parents are intelligent enough to realize that their future children will come to some harm if their lives are started. This is not a highly technical or esoteric fact, it is a fact accessible to anyone who is alive on this planet, so they should be fully aware of what they're doing. Either they are aware and are doing it intentionally, or they are unaware out of willful ignorance: neither of these options paint them in a positive light.

I am not a consequentialist. My main ethical principle, and a principle which is echoed in every system or mores or system of laws in the world, is that one has a duty not to cause harm. This is why I am committed to antinatalism.

Another objection, perhaps more attractive to people who haven't given it much thought, is to say that we take risks all the time, and that taking risks is a part of life. Certainly this is true, but the fact that our life is full of risks, some of them lethal, is precisely what the argument is about, so the objection only plays into the argument itself.

But more importantly, the risk argument pertains to *forcing other people to take risks*, not on taking risks *ourselves*. Although, again, I would gravely question the wisdom of such a decision, anyone is free to decide to play Russian Roulette, but you are not free to force someone else into it. In the same way, you are free to expose yourself to the risk of a car accident (which, given how unsafe motoring is, we all do when we go out and about) or of a crippling disease (which we do just by existing), but procreating means forcing a new person to be exposed to those risks as well.

Another misanthropic argument, the CAnCeR argument, made by Gary Mosher (a famous antinatalism advocate on the Internet), is that the life-system is basically driven by four processes:

1. *Consumption*: Living organisms need energy to keep being alive, and to do so they must consume either energy or organisms which have consumed energy.

2. *Addiction*: The compulsions to constantly seek out the things which make us feel pleasure, a sensation based on our biological needs (and which often goes off the rails in human beings, as in the case of drug addictions, gambling addictions,

shopping addictions, pornography addictions, etc).

3. *Cannibalism*: Consumption is, for the most part, a zero-sum game, and organisms can only flourish at the expense of other organisms. This is especially true of human beings, who exploit each other for the sake of their lifestyles on a massive scale.

4. *Reproduction*: How the life-system perpetuates itself over time. Successful reproduction starts the cycle all over again, and again, and again.

Lifeforms, and human societies, grow to their maximum capacity, capture and consume as many resources as they can, and, at least in the case of humans, can devastate entire ecosystems. They are a CAnCeR, an acronym which includes the four elements above.

This may seem like a bleak assessment, which does not include everything that's positive about the life-system, including its beauty and complexity, and things like love, helping each other, or the search for truth. These are common objections by people who find the antinatalist perspective "too negative."

The difference between the antinatalist perspective and the mainstream (natalist, positive) perspective is that the latter tries to erase or ignore the negative aspects of life and demands that you focus on the positives, while the former looks at everything in its proper context.

Take beauty and complexity, for example. Is it true

that the life-system is beautiful and complex? Absolutely. But neither beauty nor complexity are standard by which we can evaluate the value of a system. Beauty is a reaction of our brain to certain esthetic patterns and, while we don't understand it very well, it doesn't seem to have anything to do with moral goodness (although we commonly associate beauty with moral goodness, because both are positive traits). Complexity represents the composition of a whole into parts and the interactions between those parts, which again has no bearing on its moral goodness. A drone bomber may be extremely complex compared to a rock or a bacteria, but its victims would not call it worth creating.

As for the other factors, I am not against love, helping each other, or the search for truth. These things are necessary parts of human societies. But they are necessary only because of human needs and limitations. Love exists because we need the validation and contact given to us by other people. We help each other because we live more efficiently as a group than as individuals. We search for truth because we are ignorant of the knowledge we need in order to live and think better, in order to progress as a species. In all these cases, the negative (human needs and limitations) is primary, and the positive is the way we've found to try to palliate that negative.

I don't think that evolution is in any way "good" or that our actions are justified by CAnCeR. As I've illustrated with the Richard Dawkins quote, the natural order, an unthinking and unfeeling genetic machine, generates unimaginable suffering. The fact that the life-system is moved by these four processes does not mean that we should imitate them as rules of behavior.

Ironically, it is actually people who refuse to accept CAnCeR, who refuse to accept the basic meaninglessness and cruelty of the life-system, who have turned to evolution as their answer. Religion used to fill that role, but in Western cultures this has been found less and less adequate, and evolution has taken its place. First, we believed that man was the pinnacle of evolution, a superior creature which transcended the animal kingdom and was "specially created." When this belief was disproven by Darwin (although it is still popular today), it was replaced by the vaguely humanist concept that, since procreation is the measure of "success" in evolution, it must also be the measure of "success" in humans. It has led us to the concept of "living through our children." But this new grasping for meaning is no more valid than the religious one.

I actually do happen to think that human societies would be better off if they were organized under the lines of love, helping each other, and the search for truth (amongst other principles). The fact that some of us humans consider them important is precisely only possible when we divorce ourselves from slavish adherence to evolution as a standard of behavior.

The Asymmetry

I have already analyzed one form of asymmetry between pleasure and suffering in the form of the duty argument: we have a duty not to inflict suffering, but we do not have a duty to provide pleasure. There is another important asymmetry which has been noted by antinatalist thinkers, and that is the asymmetry between pleasure and suffering as it pertains to future lives. This asymmetry has been considered so important than when antinatalists speak of "the asymmetry," this is generally the one they're talking about.

This asymmetry has been presented both in De Giraud and Benatar's works. However, Benatar's formulation, as the most well known in the English-speaking world, has been the source of a great deal of misunderstanding. In order to present it in as clear a manner as possible, I will here present my own formulation:

(1) If a person exists, then their pain is a bad thing.
(2) If a person exists, then their pleasure is a good thing.
(3) What does not exist cannot suffer, therefore the pain in (1) is a worse deal than non-existence.
(4) What does not exist cannot be deprived of any pleasure, therefore the pleasure in (2) does not make non-existence a worse deal.
Therefore: (5) Existence is a worse deal than non-existence.

I think (1) and (2) are easily understood, but (3) and (4) create some issues for this otherwise very simple

203

argument. It is difficult for people to think of "what does not exist." One way to understand this more easily, I think, is to compare non-existence with death. After all, a person who does not exist yet is in the same state as a person who is dead (at least if one does not believe in an afterlife). Many people have made this point, including Mark Twain:

> I do not fear death. I had been dead for billions and billions of years before I was born, and had not suffered the slightest inconvenience from it.

"Dead people" (which is a figure of speech, as there is no such thing as personhood in death) don't feel or need anything. Feelings and needs are attributes of organisms that are alive. Likewise, that which does not exist has no feelings or needs, either.

So, to come back to the argument, that which does not exist cannot suffer, as it can't have feelings. This establishes the truth of premise (3). And that which does not exist cannot have needs, including the need for pleasurable experiences, therefore it cannot be deprived of those pleasurable experiences. This establishes the truth of premise (4).

To explain this even more simply: that which does not exist cannot experience stubbing its toe or suffering from tuberculosis, and that which does not exist does not lose anything from not being able to eat ice cream or win the lottery, because it doesn't need flavorful food or money.

I've spent some time on this because it is crucial that I explain this as clearly as possible, because this is where the asymmetry comes into play, and therefore where objections must attack. No one, as far as I've seen, has objections to (1) and (2) that are not mere nitpicking (e.g. some people take pleasure from "pain," which in this case really just means "actions that are painful to others"). All serious objections are directed at (3), (4), or to the structure of the argument.

The most common objection is that either (3) or (4) must be wrong because there's no good reason why the asymmetry should be true. Usually the objection is formulated against (4): the absent pleasures in (4) must somehow make non-existence a worse deal than the pleasures in (2), that is to say, the fact that what does not exist does not experience pleasures must make things worse than the fact that existing people do experience pleasures.

Even though this objection is popular, it is hard to make any sense of it. So let me take a specific example, antinatalist philosopher Julio Cabrera's use of this objection in his paper "Quality of Human Life and Non-existence (Some criticisms of David Benatar's formal and material positions)":

> ...[T]his absence [of pleasure in (4)] is bad when judged in terms of the interests of the person who would otherwise have existed. We may not know who that person would have been, but we can still say that whoever that person would have been, the avoidance

205

of his or her pleasures is bad when judged in terms of his or her potential interests.

But in order to prove (4) wrong, you have to show that the absence of pleasure is bad for something that *doesn't exist*. Even if that something is a "person who would have existed," the fact that this "non-existing person" does not get to eat ice cream is not bad for the "non-existing person." And even if that "non-existing person" came into the world, he or she could not say with a straight face that not being able to eat ice cream in their previous state of non-existence was a bad thing, any more than we would lament not being able to eat ice cream once we're dead. Have you ever seen a dead person ask for ice cream?

Attempts to refute (3) or (4) inevitably plunge into this sort of sophistry. But problems also arise when people treat the Asymmetry as being a comparison between people. Premises (3) and (4) are about non-existence, and there is really no such thing as a "non-existing person" (since personhood, by definition, implies a live, communicating organism), so the Asymmetry cannot be about comparing persons at all.

Rather, what the Asymmetry compares is state of affairs. For simplicity's sake, let me reduce the argument to one person, person X: then, (1) and (2) concern a state of affairs where person X exists, and (3) and (4) concern a state of affairs where person X does not exist. If person X exists, then their pleasures and sufferings are part of the state of affairs of the world, and if person X does not exist, then neither their pleasures nor their sufferings are part of the state of affairs of the world.

This may seem like splitting hairs, but we can observe this error in the Cabrera quote above when he talks about "the interests of the person who would otherwise have existed." There are no such interests; that which does not exist has no interests any more than it has feelings or needs. The only interests that matter are our interests and, generally speaking, those interests should hopefully include (amongst other interests) the desire to reduce suffering and maximize pleasure to ourselves and others, whether one is a utilitarian or not.

In order to further demonstrate that a pleasure that results from fulfilling a need is no better than the absence of the need itself, David Benatar discusses an argument called anti-frustrationism. Suppose we give Kate a pill that gives her the desire to see the tree closest to the Sydney Opera House be painted red. This desire is currently frustrated because that tree is not actually painted red. Now suppose we go to the Sydney Opera House, paint the tree closest to it in red, and show Kate the result. Now she might get some satisfaction out of this, but we are back to where we were before the pill: the manufactured need was created, fulfilled, and is now gone.

Now clearly the analogy is not perfect, by a long shot. For one thing, Kate exists throughout the scenario, so it doesn't compare a state of affairs where she exists and one where she does not exist.

207

But the point, I think, is clear: the state of not having the need is just as good/as bad (depending on whether you're an optimist or a pessimist, I suppose) as the pleasure that arises from fulfilling it.

But even if we go along with the objection and start from the premise that (4) is wrong, this can only lead us to a *reductio ad absurdum*. If (4) is wrong, then that which does not exist can be deprived of pleasures. This is a nonsensical statement, as anything that is deprived must necessarily exist in order to experience that deprivation. But if we assume it makes sense, it entails that failing to procreate at all times deprives some "non-existing person" of pleasure, and that any action which prevents procreation is an unethical action against those "non-existing persons." The consequence is that anyone who does not have as many children as they can is an unethical person.

I think this conclusion will be unacceptable to most people. Whether it is as unacceptable as the Asymmetry is, I suppose, a matter of personal preference. I'm willing to wager that no one who presents this objection to the Asymmetry has dedicated their lives to producing children (which would presumably involve, for men, having sex, or raping, as many women as humanly possible and, for women, being constantly pregnant for as long as they are fertile). Either way, the concept of a "non-existing person" is so absurd that it's hard to take such reasoning seriously.

If you accept the logic of the argument, then (1), (2), (3) and (4), if true, successfully demonstrate that existence is a bad deal, which is my simple way of saying that that it's morally undesirable, that no one should create it. This is why the most raised objection against the Asymmetry is against (5), the conclusion. The layman's reaction when they hear about the Asymmetry is generally something like: "but the suffering we experience is 'canceled out' by the pleasure we experience, so as long as we experience more pleasure than suffering, our life is worth it!"

I've already analyzed this argument in the previous section, and given many reasons why it fails. Comparing pleasure and suffering is mathematically impossible, suffering and pleasure do not "cancel out," not all pleasures make life worth living, and so on. Suffice it to say that, even outside of the Asymmetry, we have no logical reason to believe that some abstract balance of pleasure and suffering can make life worth living.

The Asymmetry itself is a very simple and direct argument. If you accept its structure and premises, then there is only one conclusion possible: bringing people into existence is a bad deal. When we bring a new person into the world, we create a state of affairs which is worse than the one where this person was not brought into the world.

The consent argument

I've pointed out before how we see consent as a basic ethical requirement. Some people actually believe it is the only valid ethical requirement. I disagree with such a position, but it certainly shows how important consent is. There is a strong sense that coercing people to do something is, partially or completely, wrong.

I've also pointed out how people consider children's consent irrelevant, and how this is good evidence that we treat children as means to an end. If you really care about a person, you also care about what they want or do not want for themselves.

The consent argument consists of applying this lack of consideration for consent to the act of procreation itself. Like most antinatalist arguments, it is simple and direct:

(1) Procreation entails bringing new people into the world without their consent.
(2) It is wrong to do things to others without their consent.
(3) Therefore, procreation is wrong.

If you agree with the premises, the conclusion follows logically, therefore any objection must attack the premises. But (1) is impossible to argue against, as it is a statement of fact which is easily verified and which everyone knows to be true (about themselves, at least). So the only meaningful way to attack the argument is to attack (2).

The way people go about it, generally, is to argue

something like this:

Of course it is wrong to do things to others without their consent, if they can actually consent. But in the case of a potential person, they cannot consent at all, as they do not actually exist yet. And if consent is not possible, we should simply assume it.

But this is an ad hoc rationalization, not a serious argument. People in a coma cannot consent; neither can people who are asleep, at least until they wake up. But I don't know anyone going around saying that we should do whatever we want to people in a coma or people who are asleep. So it is most definitely not true that "if consent is not possible, we should simply assume it." In fact, that's the very opposite of moral caution: if consent is not possible, then we probably should not doing to them anything they might disagree with, in short, perform an intrusive act.

A further reply here might be that bringing people into existence is a good thing, and therefore unobjectionable. But as I've previously argued, bringing people into existence is wrong, for them and for everyone else. Furthermore, there are people who believe their own existence is not a good thing (such as antinatalists), and these people prove that bringing new lives into the world is an intrusive act (for those callous enough to answer that those people should just kill themselves, I will examine the free disposal argument in the next chapter).

Ultimately, the "just assume consent" objection is a

211

might makes right argument: the potential person is utterly defenseless and cannot protect itself from being brought into this world, therefore we can do whatever we want with them. Since people have no qualms about ignoring children's consent when they exist, it makes sense that they'd care even less about the decision of bringing them into existence.

They just don't want to consider the possibility that they're actually harming actual human beings who have the right not to consent, because that would mean having to lose all their control over them. People who have some level of control over others will use any rhetoric they can to convince you that those others are not full human beings and that they are unworthy of their full human rights.

Many people are not hardcore natalists, and do believe that there should be some limits to procreation, although they all disagree on what that limit should be. They might say things like "well, having children would be fine if we didn't live in an overpopulated planet already."

On the other hand, many people try to justify procreation by stating that this world is good enough to being new people into it. But it's not their place to make that determination for another human being. There is nothing wrong with taking as much risk as you want, as long as you're taking that risk yourself, but you can't force other people to be exposed to any risk level you think is low enough (a point already made in the risk argument above).

People strongly disagree on what constitutes a "low enough" level of risk. I think there are no real life situations where everyone reasonable would agree that procreation should or should not take place, even in the extreme cases. So there is never a time when someone would be able to say that they are absolutely certain that their future children would agree with their evaluation that the world is "good enough."

Feminist antinatalism

Women are being sold a Big Lie, and more and more of them are waking up to that fact. As Hitler famously said, a colossal lie is more likely to be believed than a small lie, and the more it is repeated, the more people will lend it credibility.

The Big Lie I am referring to is the false bill of goods being sold to women by the natalists, the genderists (people who push gender roles on men and women, and the necessity of maintaining them), and even liberal feminists. It can be described as such:

Becoming a mother, along with having a career, is an essential part of being a mature, accomplished woman. It is so rewarding that you'll never regret doing it. Everything about motherhood, from pregnancy to childbirth to child-raising, is wonderful and worth doing.

In The Baby Matrix, Laura Carroll discusses the

213

myths propagated about having children. In chapter 7 of that book, she discusses what she calls the Fulfillment Assumption, the assumption that parenthood represent the ultimate path to fulfillment in life. There, she exposes the root of these myths and how they've been used specifically to bamboozle and mystify women:

> In the past, when medicine was less advanced, there were greater risks associated with both pregnancy and childbirth. Romanticized myths about pregnancy and motherhood were needed to ensure the continued survival of the family, says sociologist E.E. LeMasters. Feminist Leta Hollingsworth called these romanticized myths "illusions" and saw them as a means of social control to manipulate people to have children. The myth was emphasized, while the negatives, such as difficulties during pregnancy and childbirth, death in childbirth, or the downsides or childrearing, were not mentioned. And one of the biggest positive messages given for the mother and father was that parenthood would bring them the ultimate fulfillment in life...

> [P]owerful societal structures, such as our governments, corporations, and religious organizations have a major stake in continuing to glorify the fulfillment that comes with parenthood and children... It's in [the] best interest [of governmental, corporate, and religious factions] to keep the

population rising; the more people there are, the more taxpayers, the more products and services to sell, and the more members to contribute to the Church's power and wealth. Perpetuating the idea that parenthood is an experience you have to have in life to be truly fulfilled means more children, which ultimately serves to make these entities even more powerful.

And all mothers are part of this process of deceit. Because they know there are strong social expectations that they will extoll their motherhood, and that no one wants to hear about their problems (except close friends), they "keep a brave face" and tell people only about the positives without even considering the negatives (remind you of something?). Therefore new women do not hear anything about the suffering and lack of freedom that accompanies having a child, and so they see procreation in a favorable light.

While both genders are targeted, women are indoctrinated many orders of magnitude more than men, from their earliest childhood. We expect that girls will want to play with dolls and simulate motherhood in their play. They are told that one day they too will have children. They are taught about their "maternal instinct," which is a myth invented to justify coercing women into motherhood. Portraying stereotypes as a biological necessity is the strongest way by which bigotry can be implemented. Getting women to believe that their very biological fabric predisposes them to

215

motherhood (because women are "made" for support roles, secondary roles, passive roles) is the most powerful way to channel their energies towards achieving it.

Motherhood is very harmful to women. It can be lethally or near-lethal harmful to many (hundreds of thousands of women die every year worldwide from pregnancy and childbirth), physically harmful in some way to most (just reading about the after-effects of pregnancy alone, such as post-partum bleeding for four to six weeks, vaginal tears, fecal leakage, or incontinence, to name only those, can be hair-raising), psychiatrically harmful to some (one study done on 350,000 women saw a 72% rise in psychiatry cases after a first pregnancy[20]), and psychologically harmful to all (through stress, which is very unhealthy both mentally and physically, as well as a major loss of free time, freedom, sleep, privacy, money, and so on).

For many mothers, the expectation that motherhood is a blessed state turned into a desperate, numbing horror when came the time to actually experience it. The concept of "maternal instinct" is a lie, and many women are simply not capable of being "maternal." For these women, having to raise a child, or many children, is a personal Hell.

> "I have battled with feeling like I do not want my children from the moment my first daughter was born. Every single day is a massive struggle for me. I find myself unable to cope with my girls and I manage

by booking them into expensive child care settings / and offloading them to family whenever possible. The very minute I get them back I want them gone again and I am contemplating putting myself into a clinic of some sort whilst I get my head right. I want the kids to be taken into Foster Care until I feel like I can actually enjoy them and not dread having to look after them. I have absolutely no maternal instincts what so ever and even when the kids are hurt I find myself going through the motions without actually caring about them much. I have to remind myself to kiss them good night because this is not natural to me. I find interaction with them virtually impossible and I will take them out all of the time to avoid it."

"I love my kids – I ache for them every time I snap at them, every time I neglect their needs, turn them away because I know they deserve so much more. But I am done. I cannot make myself volunteer for one more bake sale, eat lunch at the school, go to Mcdonalds or play outside when I hate being outdoors. I'm constantly being pulled in several different directions, especially with children of such varying ages, and after almost 17 years of being called "momma" I am desperate to rediscover who I used to be before being buried under the tons and tons of mommy debris. I have tons of regrets, but I already know that my biggest one at the end of my life will be not loving what I do. I told my husband it was like living in a Communist country – being forced to work at a job you hate for your entire life. There are no easy escapes – how can one abandon their children and not feel the weight of guilt everyday? How can one continue the mind numbing endless chores of motherhood and not want to run away? All I can do is accept this is the life I have – but accepting isn't the same as enjoying and I can honestly say everyday I hate what I do without a ton of guilt (there is still some residual guilt)."

"I constantly feel that if only someone had told me the truth, I would have spared myself and my husband this miserable life, and could have spared two beautiful children this disgusting world."

"I don't know why, but it's gotten worse these last few months...to the point where my misery is so encompassing it's all I can think about. Sometimes the sadness weighs so heavily on me it's physically challenging to do simple day to day things. It's all I can do to get through my work day (I have a full time job) followed by picking the kids up at the sitters, feeding them dinner, giving them baths (my least favorite time of the day!! Ugh, bathtime = torture), going through the bedtime rituals and then, enjoying an hour to myself during which I eat junk food and watch crap TV before passing out on the couch and having to force myself to go upstairs to bed. Such quality me time.

I've always had suicidal thoughts, but it seems like more and more lately my suicidal fantasies take up so much of my time. One night last month I went home and put the kids to bed and thought, "tonight is the night." And obviously I didn't do it...but I was so consumed by my own depression that I couldn't see going on another day. It's the only thing I can think of doing that will put an end to my pain."

"I empathize with every mother here who believed what the media portrayed and others told them about how amazing it was to be a mom. I too fell for it. I am now hating life and everything that comes with being a mom. I understand I became a mother for all the wrong reasons and I OWN my decision and the consequences. I will say that I have written off all those so called "friends" who made me feel like I was missing out on the best experience in life and how much I would regret not having kids. These were not my friends, these were miserable women who wanted miserable company. Not to say that every women is miserable, but I KNOW some of these so called "friends" defiantly lied. I feel these are the same women who sit on this site and say how the Childfree women on here are just trying to rub it in the rest of our faces and that they have other social issues/deformities and to get off the forum (just an FYI if you are socially incompetent you are socially incompetent regardless of your kid status). The women who say this crap are just jealous of the childfree's lifestyle (I'm sure I'll get some defensive mothers writing back to counteract that statement), but I understand you ladies aren't here for that reason, you have people around you telling you how great it is and are on the fence about having a child and are just trying to see all sides of the spectrum. I understand and am here to tell you it isn't as great as some of your friends and family are telling you. Of course it is up to you, but know that it is 100 times harder then what society makes it out to be."

These are only a few short extracts from the personal stories of a number of mothers who contributed to the web site Secret Confessions, an anonymous site where people can post their stories or reply to past stories.

I grant that, since the stories are anonymous, there's no way to confirm them. The testimonies given there are no more or less reliable than any other testimony. They are certainly more reliable than testimonies about the joys of motherhood, since people generally have far more incentive in confirming generally accepted ideas than going against them. There are no rewards for people who denounce motherhood (not even amongst feminists, despite the false stereotype that feminists loathe motherhood).

I imagine many people who have not thought about their own indoctrination very much would refuse to listen to such stories because these are "exceptions," freaks of nature, and say something like "these people just need major psychiatric help." Such profound disgust is natural, as we are indoctrinated to believe that motherhood is part of what makes a woman, and that without it a woman is necessarily broken or immature.

The fact is that these women are not broken or immature. They are perfectly normal and their reaction is that of a person thrust into a situation they were grossly misinformed about and which ends up profoundly clashing with their personality. They simply do not have that spark that we're taught happens to all mothers, that bond that supposedly binds mothers to their children, which arises from their "maternal instinct."

It is not my intention, however, to overstate the case. I have no doubt that there are many mothers who are well suited to motherhood and child-raising (however morally repugnant these tasks are), not because of their gender or anything innate, but because of their personalities and interests. These women just happen to be "lucky" to live in a society where their personality roughly lines up with what is socially expected of them.

But whatever you think about those women, the fact

221

is that they, too, were lied to. We were all lied to. My argument is not "no woman could ever be happy as a mother," but that the institutions in our Western societies lie to us in order to maintain a population growth which is in accordance with their interests. These lies go against feminist values because they aim to restrict women's ambitions and personal freedom, and for the benefit of institutions which are mostly ruled by men and which function according to patriarchal values.

As Simone de Beauvoir wrote in The Second Sex:

> [P]regnancy is above all a drama playing itself out in the woman between her and herself. She experiences it both as an enrichment and a mutilation; the fetus is part of her body, and it is a parasite exploiting her; she possesses it, and she is possessed by it... [S]nared by nature, she is plant and animal, a collection of colloids, an incubator, an egg...

Pregnancy is a form of objectification, in that it uses a woman's organs and energy for a purpose which is not guided by her own determination, that of growing a fetus. It transforms a human being into a machine, a walking incubator. Motherhood diverts women's energies and freedom into raising children instead of pursuing their own welfare. All of this goes directly against the feminist programme and is a result of the patriarchal exploitation of women's creative energies.

Furthermore, domestic violence, another crucial feminist issue, is closely linked to the rate of unwanted pregnancies. Many women are simply forced or cajoled (or both) into having unwanted children by abusive husbands.

I've just discussed patriarchal exploitation of women's procreative labor. Some speculate that that this exploitation may be the origin of sexism itself. In her book The Creation of Patriarchy, Gerda Lerner discusses the idea that patriarchy began as control over women for the purposes of procreation. If this is true, then procreation holds a place of choice in the anti-feminist pantheon. It is no surprise that all anti-feminist ideologies hold that a woman's place is in the home, barefoot and pregnant.

Based on this, one could argue that feminism, fully understood, cannot be expressed without at the same time attacking natalist premises, especially the implicit premise that women's main purpose is to perpetuate the species. Furthermore, pushing for procreation makes women as a class dependent on men for genetic material, for resources, for support. This is contrary to the need for the kind of physical and intellectual independence that could emancipate women.

Another feminist argument against procreation is that procreation wastes women's productive energies. Not only that, but it wastes them in far greater proportion than it does men's: not only do women do the physical labor of carrying the fetus, but they do a majority of the child-rearing work as well. This means that women are less free to devote their energies to real accomplishments (whatever those might be), or do anything else they value. It means they are being held down by having children. Only rich women are able to delegate the time costs of child-raising to other people, generally to other women. Either way, child-raising requires an incredible amount of attention, time and resources which women could use for much better ends.

As Isaac Asimov answered to a question on Bill Moyers' show World of Ideas:

> As long as you have women under conditions where they don't feel any sense of value or self-worth except as mothers, they'll have a lot of children because that's the only way they can prove they're worth something. In general, if you look through the world, the lower the status of women, the higher the birth rate, and the higher the birth rate, the lower the status of women. If you could raise the status of women, I am certain the birth rate would fall drastically through the choice of the women themselves. We're always saying that there's no fulfillment like having children, but I notice mostly it's men who say that. You know, men get along without giving birth to children. They do that by finding other things to do. If women could find other things to do, too, they would have fewer children.

I do not mean to say that mothers should be blamed for refusing to use their energies in a constructive manner. It's important to remember here that mothers are also the victims of the lies propagated about motherhood. The responsibility of not procreating and generally lowering the harm we inflict on others belongs to all of us. But mothers are still disproportionately affected compared to fathers precisely because child raising is still considered "women's work," which is why I classify it as a feminist argument.

I've discussed socialization as it relates to pedagogy previously, and how it is mainly a function of society and not of the parents. This presents a particular problem for feminists: no matter how they raise their children, their child will become a member of the oppressor class (men as a class) or of the oppressed class (women as a class). Men as a class are, in an overwhelming majority, the perpetrators of violent crimes (90%+ of most categories of violent crimes are committed by men, against men and women) and women as a class are overwhelmingly the victims of rape and sexual assault. This means that any child may grow up to be a perpetrator of sexual crimes or a victim of sexual crimes, depending on their gender.

I will present another version of this problem, based on Christianity, in the next chapter. But basically, the argument is simple: the more children that are created, the more people exist who will be indoctrinated into gender roles, re-enact their cruelties, and, ultimately, defend them. The fewer

225

people there are in the world, the fewer such cruelties will exist.

While I think all these arguments are important, we also have to look at the big picture. Every single institution which depends on, and pushes, the pro-procreation party line is also anti-feminist in nature, most notably capitalism, nationalism and religion. Capitalism needs population growth or new markets in order to fulfill its need for endless expansion. Nationalism needs population growth in order to maintain the power and tax base of the nation. Religion needs population growth in order to entrap more people into its indoctrination through the family structure.

In all this, what is not being considered is the well-being and freedom of women themselves. As I said before, natalism entails ignoring the values and experiences of women, like how childism entails ignoring the values and experiences of children. As Karl Pilkington wrote in his book The Moaning of Life about making children being justified as a "life-changing experience":

> Losing a leg is a life-changing experience, but that doesn't mean you'd actually want to lose one. 'Oh, but you're missing out,' they say, as if they know what I want more than I do. Would they say to a gay bloke, 'Oh, you should get your hands on a nice pair of tits, you'd love it, mate'?"

Chapter 6
Objections to antinatalism

The Non-Identity Problem

I've mentioned the Non-Identity Problem (NIP) many times because it is the linchpin of any position which seeks to undermine antinatalism. It is a fairly reasonable argument, and, if true, would undermine the whole enterprise of this book, which is to expose the child and woman sides of the triangle of procreation. If the NIP is true, then there can be no child side of the triangle.

The argument is very simple: future persons do not exist, therefore it is meaningless to speak of their rights or states of being. And if that's the case, then it is meaningless to say things like "procreation fails to take into account the values of the child" or "it is better not to have been" (to borrow the name of Benatar's book). How can it be better not to be, if future persons do not have states of being to compare with actual persons? How can procreation take into account values that do not exist?

There are three major answers to the NIP.

1. Objection from causal linkage

This objection consists of saying that the NIP is really just a semantics game, and that it serves to obscure the cause and effect relationship between the intent to procreate, fetuses, and children. In order to illustrate this, let me use the analogy of a machine being built in a factory.

Suppose that an engineer is supervising the manufacture of a new piece of factory equipment, which is expected to produce some sort of finished product, let's say computers. Someone else pours over the blueprints and come up to the engineer and tells him that the equipment will produce defective computers that will short-circuit on their users.

Now, if the engineer replied to this by saying, "your warning is completely useless because the defective products don't exist yet, therefore there's no point in talking about it right now," what would we think of such a response? We would think it to be bizarre, because the causal chain between the error in the blueprint and the defective computers is clear to us, and the fact that the defective computers do not yet exist has no bearing on it. They may not exist at that moment, but they will exist eventually, if the project is completed.

Likewise, if the defective computers end up killing someone, we would not come to the conclusion that the engineer or the factory are not responsible because the computers did not exist at the time. As long as one can prove that they were aware of the defect, they would be held responsible. This is just simple logic.

Any future child does not exist right now, by definition. But we know that children will be born in the future, as they have been born for as long as humanity has existed. And we can predict that those children will live similar kinds of lives to those that have been lived in the past, or those we live right now. They will live in the same world we live in, and like us they will have desires, values and feelings. That's all we need to establish in order to talk about the children's side of the procreation triangle.

We can put this in the context of a fetus, as well. We generally believe that women shouldn't drink or take drugs while they're pregnant. But why should this be the case? After all, the fetus (at least early on in the pregnancy) is not a person, it's only a future person. Sure, the fetus is an actual physical object, but it's not a person. It has no interests or values. If the NIP is correct, we cannot make any causal connection between a person and something that is not a person yet, and that includes fetuses. But that goes against everything we know on the subject.

One further confirming piece of evidence is that NIP-style arguments aren't used in any other field of inquiry or scientific discipline. For example, we think it makes perfect sense to talk about concerns regarding how damage to the environment will affect future generations, even though those future generations don't exist yet. No one pipes up to say, "those future generations you're talking about don't exist yet, so they have no values and interests, and it makes no sense to talk about 'their lives' being affected by future conditions." If they did, their argument would be called nonsensical.

Likewise, no one talks about a physicist's prediction about an experiment as being useless because the experiment hasn't happened yet. No one comes up to a physicist and says "well, your paper about this theoretical particle is stupid because there's no point in talking about a particle that we don't know exists yet." Again, that would just be silly.

Based on this, it is clear to me that people who use the NIP are disingenuous debaters. I highly doubt that any of them would be willing to use the NIP in any other context but antinatalism.

2. The NIP doesn't actually apply to most antinatalism arguments

The NIP is usually brought up in response to the Asymmetry. Remember that the Asymmetry compares the suffering and pleasure contained in two states of affairs: one where a person X exists and one where that person X does not exist. It is not a comparison between two individuals (one which exists and one which does not exist), but a comparison of two states of affairs. Neither side of the Asymmetry is concerned with the state of a future person.

To make this clearer, imagine a person who is deciding whether to commit suicide. What exactly are they comparing? They are not comparing their current state with the state of their future dead self, for there is no such thing as a "dead self" (selfhood only applies to living organisms). No, I imagine that they are looking at their anticipated future, and thinking whether they would rather have that or end their life at that moment: basically, comparing the state of their life (so far) to the anticipated life they might lead if it continues.

In both cases, we're not comparing people, but states of affairs. Neither the antinatalist nor the suicide base their argument on the state of future/dead persons. If the concept of suicide makes sense (regardless of your position about it), then there's no reason why the concept of antinatalism wouldn't make as much sense. The main difference in both examples is that we're flipping the order of existence and non-existence: in the case of birth, we go from a state where person X does not exist to a state where person X begins to exist, while in the case of suicide we go from a state where person X exists to a state where person X no longer exists.

3. Objection from basic moral talk

I have already argued that the NIP makes discussion of any future-talk impossible. This fact has another far-reaching consequence. Take any mundane moral statement, such as "you shouldn't punch Robert in the face" (note that whatever position you hold on meta-ethics is irrelevant here). It seems very clear: if you uphold this moral principle to me, and I then go and punch Robert in the face, you would find this reprehensible.

But if I was a proponent of the NIP, I could then reply something like this:

"When you said that, neither future-me (the person who punched) or future-Robert (the person who got punched) existed. So your principle couldn't possibly have applied to either of them, as it's pointless to talk about people that don't yet exist. At best, your principle only applied to me and Robert at the exact moment you said the sentence. Anything else is gibberish."

I don't expect you to agree with this reply, as it is absolutely insane. But it is perfectly in line with the NIP. The only reason why we can say that my present self and my future self are the same person is because we acknowledge the causal linkage between them. I know I am the same person than the me from five, ten or twenty years ago because I know that my selves in the past are the cause of my current self.[21]

As I discussed, the NIP denies the possibility of causal linkage. It cannot connect a future person to an actual person, or a blueprint to a machine. If it cannot do that, then it cannot recognize a present self and a future self as the same person, either.

Another consequence of the NIP is that we cannot make an meaningful statement about fictional persons, since after all fictional persons do not actually exist. For instance, most people in Western countries would agree with the statement "Santa Claus is fat and jolly," even though there really is no such person as Santa Claus (if you still believed in Santa Claus until now, then I apologize for breaking the bad news). Although this objection does not apply specifically to the way NIP is used against antinatalism, it further highlights its contradictions with reality. Talk of fictional persons is so important in our daily lives that any arguments which denies its existence should be rather suspicious, to say the least.

Purpose-creation as a rebuttal to antinatalism

An obvious objection to antinatalism is that some other ideology gives our lives purpose, and that this purpose is more important than the arguments or ethical imperatives I've discussed in the previous chapter.

People disagree vastly on what life's purpose is. To a lot of people, God gives our lives purpose, and that specific purpose (doing God's will) is dependent on how one interprets religious doctrine. As I've discussed before, some people who confuse the theory of evolution with a substitute god think that the purpose of life is to reproduce in order to perpetuate one's genetic makeup, which is a rather abstract concept which cannot really be perpetuated by a purely physical process. Some ideologically-motivated egoists may tell you that the purpose of life is to have the most power.

But if you ask most people, who don't think too much about such abstract and useless questions, they will probably tell you one of two things: that the purpose of life is to be happy, or that the purpose of life is to help others.

I've already discussed how natalism brings with it a different kind of purpose to life, one that is purely economical in nature. To natalists, we should be brought into this world in order to make numbers go up or make numbers go down. There is no real reason to exist, just statistics. This is a rather bleak view of human existence.

Even though I don't think most people really consider the issue in much depth, I do think that purpose and meaning are important parts of the way our society functions. Meaning, after all, is the way we build purpose. For example, in order to have the purpose of "being happy," we need to construct the meanings of what happiness is, how you know you're happy, how you acquire and keep it, what ways to be happy or to express happiness are acceptable or desirable in one's society. And every point on this list relies on a whole network of meanings, both personal and social.

According to one theory in social psychology, terror management theory, human cultures exist to provide life with meaning, which serves to counter the fear of death. All our major institutions (religion, government, the family, the arts, and so on) serve to provide meaning through making the individual feel that they are a part of something greater than themselves, an extension of themselves, like how many parents believe they live on through their children.

I called this section purpose-creation. No doubt many people (especially religious believers) will object that surely we don't create the purpose of life. If we did, it would be wholly useless. The purpose of life must be something that exists outside of us, that we must discover. Other people would disagree and state that everyone can have their own purpose if they want to, that it is individual lives that have purpose and not human life as a whole.

I am personally unconvinced by the religious arguments. I argued for an order/value gap in chapter 4, and it applies here as well: divine orders about what our life's purpose is, or should be, have no relevance to what it actually is. But there is also some reason to doubt the other account: if we can all just make up our own personal meaning, then it seems that a person's choice of purpose tells us something about that person but absolutely nothing about human life itself. Such a purpose seems no more relevant to antinatalism than one's preferences in color combinations or ice cream flavors.

I do concede that a majority of people think their lives have a purpose, although not nearly all (one study found that only 60% of Americans reported having a life purpose[22]). I believe there are two ways antinatalism meets this challenge. The first is, as I've done, to show that this purpose is either invalid or merely a personal preference, and therefore irrelevant to antinatalism. The second is to argue that this purpose does not address antinatalism, because it assumes the necessity of procreation in the first place. Therefore, using such purpose as an argument is circular.

Again, let me start with the position that we are alive in order to be happy. Are people who exist justified in seeking happiness? Of course. But antinatalism is not concerned with the justifications of existing people. It is concerned with procreation, starting new lives. People try to be happy because happiness is a good feeling and they always have the potential to be unhappy. The feeling and the potential only exist because they exist. Therefore they cannot justify procreation.

If someone said, "I want to give birth to a new human being because I want them to be happy," then the obvious reply would be that this is circular reasoning, because it assumes the necessity of bringing new people into the world. Without that necessity, we can only conclude that there is no reason to bring into existence a new being who has the need to be happy, just so that need can be fulfilled. The end result (happiness) only exists because of the presence of a need (the need to not be unhappy, the need to experience positive feelings), and there is no reason for that need to exist in the first place.

We can easily demonstrate, by taking humanity as a whole instead of just single individuals, that there can be no purpose to procreation. Such a purpose cannot arise from human moral concerns, because without humanity there are no human moral concerns in the first place. It cannot arise from human needs, because without humanity there are no human needs. Without humanity, there is nothing to ground any human justification on. Any human truth, any human principle, any human evaluation, requires the existence of human beings. And any truth, principle or evaluation which is not human has no relevance to us as biological organisms.

You may think, why argue from humanity as a whole? We are all born as individuals, not as "humanity." My point is that it exposes the circularity of the purposes we attribute to each other: they are only convincing because we are only looking at one particular life in the context of other lives. If valid, all they could prove is that a given human life is desirable given the existence of other lives. But if all procreation is unjustified to begin with, then the point is moot.

Another major objection can be raised against religious purpose specifically. Suppose Christianity is correct and that God exists and judges all humans as worthy of eternal salvation or eternal torture (or annihilation, according to some denominations), then we can deduce that one's children may, as a definite possibility, end their lives in eternal torture or annihilation, which in either case means an infinite negative. And if this is the case, then procreation is the most evil action possible.

When Christian breeders create a new human life, they know for a fact that this life might end up in Hell or annihilated, instead of going to Heaven. Sure, they might delude themselves into thinking that the chance is so low as to be negligible, or that they're going to "raise them right" so it never happens, but they know the risk exists. And by definition infinity cannot be divided by any finite number. No matter what the percentage of responsibility of the parents is, it's definitely more than zero. And any percentage means that they are responsible for an infinity of suffering.

The belief in Hell is cruel and inhumane (not to mention it's not even Biblical). Anyone who seriously believes in Hell is a cruel and inhumane person, no matter what else they may believe in. They believe that any human being, no matter what they've done, may deserve eternal torture simply for not holding one particular belief amongst thousands of equally likely beliefs. What they may not like to think about, is that this conclusion also applies to their own children.

Keep in mind that we universally consider murder to be evil, and yet murder is a finite negative (the victim only loses the remaining life they would have had otherwise, not an eternity of bliss). Simply for having a child, Christian breeders are infinitely more guilty than murderers. A perfectly good Christian couple who goes to church every week and gives money to charity, and have a child, are automatically more evil than a million Jeffrey Dahmers. This may seem like an absurd conclusion, but it is the logical result of an absurd belief system.

Obviously I don't believe in Hell, and I don't believe that all Christian breeders are infinitely evil. But it brings into question the belief that God gives purpose to human beings. No matter what religious denomination you choose, most people on the planet are not part of it, so most people on the planet are wrong. How can this divine purpose be universal (which it needs to be in order to justify procreation), or even adequate, when so many human beings fail to grasp it at a very basic level? At least "we exist to be happy" or "we exist to help others" are universally applicable.

The belief in Hell has not stopped Christians from procreating, in accordance with the Genesis order to "be fruitful and multiply." Christians throughout history have believed that it was women's duty to pump out children (and some still do, such as Quiverfull protestants, and Catholics in many countries). This merely proves that Christianity is a profoundly contradictory belief system, and that believers don't mind it because they don't become Christians for rational reasons. They are free to believe that their specific form of religious belief provides them with a reason to breed, but we are free to disbelieve them, as well. At any rate, I think it should be clear, to anyone who is not already a believer, that Christian belief entails anti-natalist conclusions in a profound sense.

The Ice Cream salespeople

Another popular argument against antinatalism consists of saying that the pleasures of life are so important that we should want to bring new people into this world. The nature of the pleasure depends on the person arguing for them: they will usually invoke things like sunsets, love, family (which seems a little circular), and so on.

I call these people the Ice Cream salesmen because they are basically trying to sell us the life-system based on these relatively trivial matters. They are basically a modern version of snake oil peddlers, promising that this or that remedy will cure all your ills, but with the caveat that even snake oil peddlers didn't have the arrogance of believing that they could cure the ills of everyone in the world.

Now, first of all, I am not denying that there are plenty of pleasures in most people's lives. As Westerners, we are prone to vastly exaggerating the importance of those pleasures (e.g. because we delegate a lot of our suffering to people in third world countries and thus can consume more products and have more time to experience leisure), but they are an important part of our lives. I certainly wouldn't want to live without love, orgasms, good food, the pleasure of intellectual pursuits, and so on and so forth.

However, it's important to put these things in their proper context. As I've discussed in the section about the Asymmetry, only people who exist can be deprived of pleasures. You can, for example, ground a child and deprive them of dinner or their video games or whatever else. But you can't deprive non-existence of anything. There is nothing in the universe that suffers from the fact that billions more human beings could exist right now and eat ice cream, look at sunsets, and so on.

Unlike natalists, who simply ignore the impact of suffering on procreation, antinatalists consider both sides of the story, pleasure and suffering. Their conclusion is that while pleasures are necessary (and desirable) for people who exist, they do not in themselves justify bringing new lives into this world.

There is only way in which we can make the Ice Cream argument work: by positing some kind of pre-human entity (like a soul or a space foetus, like in the movie 2001: A Space Odyssey) floating around in space suffering from being deprived of earthly pleasures. While this idea may make sense to Scientologists or some other New Age believers, it makes no sense scientifically. No matter what your position is on the abortion issue, I think we can at least all agree that new human lives do not start in outer space.

Ice Cream salesmen do not get this far in their thinking, if they think about it at all: they just think that, because they enjoy certain parts of life, that by giving birth to new persons they are giving them the "gift" of experiencing these parts of life. This, however, makes no sense if we include the consideration already discussed. How can something be a "gift" if the "gift" is of absolutely no benefit to the recipient? If I take away X (the lack of deprivation) and replace it with a different but equal value Y (the pleasure), I have not given

241

you a gift, I have made a forced exchange (or as a less charitable commentator might say, a theft followed by an unwanted substitution). The best we can say is that the "chance" of experiencing these pleasures does not, in itself, leave one worse off than they were before, but it's no "gift."

"Life is a gift" is not a very good metaphor. A better metaphor might be that life is a draft that spares no one, for a war that only benefits the elite. Higher procreation rates benefit social institutions like corporations, religions, and governments. They are a great detriment to the average person, because they mean less resources available, less desirable land and space available, higher crime rates (crime being proportional to population density), more interpersonal friction and conflict, fewer jobs, generally less freedom.

Again, the fact that our lives have a lot of pleasures is not under question. What is under question is the relevance of that fact to procreation.

Some people, not understanding this point, continue to object by saying that we antinatalists demand that the world be perfect, that we are basically whiners who have some sort of grudge against life because it's not all pleasure all the time, and that we are the ones who lack perspective.

I personally find this argument ludicrous because a perfect world, one without suffering, would also be a world without pleasure, and therefore a world not worth living in at all. It's important to keep in mind that pleasure and suffering are both dependent on the existence of human needs. When we fulfill our biological or psychological needs, we experience pleasure; when we fail to fulfill them, we experience suffering. A world without suffering is necessarily a world without needs, and therefore without pleasure.

By and large, antinatalists are against suffering. I think it fair to say that this is a central pillar of the ideology. But they are also realistic about the amount of suffering in the world. I don't think the world could ever be "perfect," neither do I think that it should be. While I appreciate any good-natured effort to reduce suffering, I hold no illusions of eradicating it.

The free disposal argument

The expression "free disposal" as applied to suicide is very old: it harkens back to am essay from David Hume called Of Suicide, where he states the following (bold mine):

> All animals are entrusted to their own prudence and skill for their conduct in the world, and have full authority, as far as their power extends, to alter all the operations of nature. Without the exercise of this authority, they could not subsist a moment. Every action, every motion of a man innovates in the order of some parts of matter, and diverts, from their ordinary

course, the general laws of motion. Putting together, therefore, these conclusions, we find, that human life depends upon the general laws of matter and motion, and that 'tis no encroachment on the office of providence to disturb or alter these general laws. **Has not every one, of consequence, the free disposal of his own life?** And may he not lawfully employ that power with which nature has endowed him?...

Were the disposal of human life so much reserved as the peculiar province of the almighty that it were an encroachment on his right for men to dispose of their own lives; it would be equally criminal to act for the preservation of life as for its destruction. If I turn aside a stone, which is falling upon my head, I disturb the course of nature, and I invade the peculiar province of the almighty, by lengthening out my life, beyond the period, which, by the general laws of matter and motion, he had assigned to it.

I quoted Hume extensively here to show the general thrust of his argument: that he uses the concept of "free disposal" to mean that suicide is, logically, not prohibited by the will of God. He makes the point that, if suicide was an inference in God's plan, then so would saving someone's life. He wasn't making any point about procreation.

Bryan Caplan, the natalist economist, uses the term "free disposal" in a somewhat different manner; he uses it to argue against antinatalism. His argument is ridiculously simplistic:

> We know that people almost universally prefer existing to not existing because there are so many cheap and easy ways to stop existing.

Basically, what he is saying is that anyone who is unhappy with their lives can just go kill themselves, and anyone who does not kill themselves are clearly happy about their lives, because they have access to "free disposal." He uses this reasoning to argue the proposition that it is better to exist.

There are so many things wrong with this "argument": none of it makes any sense or connects logically to any other point. Let me deconstruct it in order to demonstrate this:

1. There are "cheap and easy" ways to stop existing.
2. Anyone who preferred not existing to existing would make themselves stop existing.
3. The vast majority of people do not make themselves stop existing.
4. Therefore the vast majority of people prefer existence to non-existence.

Each premise here is completely false:

1. Suicide always comes with a heavy cost- not just in the risk of failing and ending up in an even worse state, but also at a cost to one's family, friends, and society. Until suicide becomes legal and

245

commercial means arise for its provision (such as the famous Swiss non-profit organization Dignitas, although their services are still expensive), suicide will never be "cheap and easy."

2. Because there are heavy costs associated to suicide, killing oneself is highly unlikely to be a person's automatic reaction to preferring not to exist. Also, the right to die is not recognized in most places, and we are subjected to fairly heavy anti-suicide indoctrination, so a lot of people will reject suicide off hand, even if they don't want to live (compare to the great number of unwanted children who are not aborted because abortion is illegal or stigmatized). Few institutions stand to benefit from supporting suicide, except for the assisted suicide of people with debilitating illnesses (which is why governments are starting to come around to allowing this to happen, not out of compassion but out of economic incentives).

But furthermore, there is no clear reason why a preference for non-existence would necessarily entail a desire to stop existing. I think non-existence is always better, for reasons already discussed, but I do not desire to stop existing.

I already touched on this when analyzing the question "if you hate life so much, why don't you kill yourself?" Then, I pointed out that this question relies on an equivocation between two meanings of life, the life-system and one's individual lifespan. If we correctly label both, the question becomes "if you hate the life-system so much, why don't you

246

end your lifespan?" But there is no clear correlation between the two. Most of us, antinatalists or not, have values, desires, relationships, and ongoing concerns which make our own lifespan worth living, regardless of our opinion about the life-system.

3. This is superficially correct. However, for the reasons I pointed out in response to premise 2, this does not prove anything about people's happiness, life satisfaction, or their desire to exist. But more importantly, it is impossible for us (e.g. you, the reader, as well as myself at the time I write this) to "stop existing," in the sense that we exist at this present moment and that fact cannot be erased. We may prefer "non-existence," but anyone who was born and exists cannot attain "non-existence." At best, we can die, but dying merely stops existence. The only way to be part of "non-existence" is to never have been born.

Which leads us to the conclusion, proposition 4. Do most people prefer existence to non-existence? Actually, I doubt anyone has any opinion about such an esoteric question, except the few people who have been exposed to antinatalism (either pro or con), or maybe some nerdy metaphysicians trying to create their own religion.

Now, most people don't want to die, but, as I pointed out, that's an entirely different issue. Most importantly, we can't tell how many people want to die simply by looking at suicide rates, because the vast majority of people who want to die will not commit suicide.

Caplan doubles down on his irrational argument by invoking the notion of consent:

> It's OK to create people as long as they would consent beforehand. How can you know? You can't be sure, but [arguments] show that almost everyone would consent if they could. That's good enough.

I already discussed the consent argument and the standard reply that we should just assume consent. But his reply also assumes that people's desires is a good indication of what a "non-existing person" would desire. That's a very dubious point, and he doesn't even try to back it up. We have no particular reason to believe that "almost everyone," in a state prior to existence and knowing how their life would turn out, would choose to come into existence. This is all purely hypothetical anyway, and simply could not support the argumentative load that Caplan blithely thinks it can, even if he could prove it.

Suppose we concede the whole point and assume the proposition that "most people prefer existence to non-existence." What does this prove exactly? It certainly does not prove that existence is better than non-existence, which is what would be required to argue against antinatalism. All that Caplan could possibly prove with this argument is that most people would reject antinatalism if they were presented with it. Not a particularly surprising or informative conclusion (any antinatalist could have told him that right away, eliminating the need to make up this whole spurious argument). But the popularity of an idea or belief system has little to do with its truth or falsity, anyway.

But even if the argument could somehow prove that existence is preferable, it would fall into the same problem as anti-Asymmetry arguments: proving that existence is inherently superior entails that procreation is always good and refraining from procreating is always bad. This is not the conclusion that Caplan wants you to arrive at: he wants you to believe that procreation is morally blameless, not that we should impose procreation on everyone, but his argument fails at doing that.

While antinatalists support suicide as (amongst other reasons) the last and most effective means people have to spare themselves from continued suffering, they are not under any obligation to commit suicide themselves. In a similar way, we are not, and cannot be, under any obligation to murder other people, even though doing so might alleviate some future suffering. Antinatalists do not single out individual lives as the problem, but a worldview (natalism and natalist premises in our culture) which promotes procreation as a means to alleviate social problems or support social institutions which depend on population growth. No one's suicide or murder can change that.

A related argument to "why don't you kill yourself?", and one which is equally relevant to this argument, is "what if you hadn't been born?" This is

249

an attempt to get the other person to admit that existence is important because we all want to exist. But this is, again, a complete misunderstanding. Surely most people who exist value their own existence, but this is just a personal opinion which proves nothing about whether existence as a whole is more desirable or less desirable.

I certainly would rather not have been born, for the reasons described in the previous chapter. I think it is better, on the whole, for anyone to not have been born. But we, who were born, are the unfortunate ones. As David Benatar wrote, "nobody is lucky enough not to be born, everybody is unlucky enough to have been born- and particularly bad luck it is."

Ecological antinatalism and mainstream environmentalism

There is one group of people which has led the charge against the impact of overpopulation on humans and the environment, and that's the mainstream environmentalist movement. Clearly the movement is not antinatalist in any way, so there is some good reason there to examine environmentalism from an antinatalist perspective.

Because it is a mainstream movement, it depends vitally on supporting the natalist order for its credibility. That means that mainstream environmentalism, despite its name, cannot offer effective solutions for the degradation of the environment. The sort of solutions they advocate, like reforestation, recycling, alternative energy sources, and so on, are all necessary but do not provide a solution because population growth will always outpace such measures. Statistically, having a child dwarfs any measure taken to reduce one's carbon footprint by at least an order of magnitude, partially because most children will end up having more children. This is a highly significant fact, in that it demonstrates that any attempt at reducing the carbon footprint of humanity is doomed to failure in the long run unless population itself is reduced.

Ecological antinatalism, on the other hand, recognizes the necessity of grappling with the undesirability of procreation in order to make any headway against the accelerating degradation of the environment and depletion of our natural heritage. While the other forms of antinatalism I've discussed also question procreation, ecological antinatalism does so by looking at all life on this planet, instead of concentrating on humans. It is a global perspective on suffering.

Antinatalism is not solely concerned about human suffering. You may recall the Dawkins quote about the amount of suffering in nature being beyond our capacity to imagine. If we are to be serious about examining procreation, then that suffering also needs to be taken seriously, if only because the creation of new humans necessarily involves increasing this mind-boggling amount of suffering. We massacre animals and their habitats in order to make space for humans. We torture them in factory farms in order to feed ourselves, and coerce them to reproduce. We also mistreat them as pets.

Some may argue that animals are not kind to each other, either. After all, most of the "unimaginable suffering" I've discusses has to do with predation from other species (including bacteria and viruses), not from humans. That is a true statement, and a problem for mainstream environmentalism, but it only improves the antinatalist case: it shows that the fundamental problem is the reproduction of sentience. Freeing animals and preserving their habitats would be a good first step, but it will not, by far, end the suffering of other species on this planet.

Others, more uncaring, may ask: why care about other species at all? Here we must make distinctions. While far more sophisticated than we commonly believe, trees and other plants still cannot feel pain or experience sentience. Microscopic organisms or insects do not feel pain, either. On the other side of the scale, neuroscientists are in general agreement that mammals and birds, as well as some other animals like octopuses, are sentient and can feel pain. The rest is somewhat contentious.

Now, I am not advocating against trees or microscopic organisms, which are both vitally important to life on this planet, but rather that they lie outside the purview of environmental antinatalism. But once we have established that there are numerous other species that experience suffering, I don't think a case can be made for human suffering being more important than any other form of animal suffering. The beliefs that humans were specially created by God or qualitatively superior to all other animals have been disproven by the theory of evolution.

Often it is argued that antinatalism is a far too "extreme" position, and that what we really need is population control, which is portrayed as a "moderate" position. If only we could stabilize the population, all our problems would be resolved.

While I don't deny that spreading the belief that we should consciously control population growth through political means would be highly beneficial, it also misses the point because it assumes that procreation in itself is not questionable and reduces the issue to a matter of who decides the quantity of procreation that will occur (parents or society). It implies that, as long as an act of procreation receives the support of society, it is a good act. Antinatalism rejects this premise and puts forward the claim that acts of procreation must be viewed as morally wrong by default.

The solution of population control also does not address the suffering that other species inflict on each other. Since it is unable to deal with the wide scope of suffering in the world, population control cannot be an alternative to antinatalism. At best it is an alternative to certain specific forms of antinatalism.

Some may argue that at least population control is a more practical alternative to antinatalism, but this is far from obvious. For one thing, practicality does not apply to ethical propositions: antinatalism (i.e. the position that procreation is wrong) is either true or false, but it cannot be more or less practical.

Arguments about practicality usually revolve around the belief that antinatalism implies the extinction of humanity. What they're really saying is that population control is more practical than human extinction. But it is silly to say that antinatalism could bring about human extinction, if only because there will always be people who will breed regardless of social pressure (just as there will always be people who will refuse to breed regardless of social pressure). There is no realistic risk of antinatalism going "too far."

If anything, it is the people who promote population control who do not go far enough, for population control will always be an unrealistic position unless it also attacks the premise of "reproductive rights" and the strong sense of entitlement that people have towards having children. People who have a privilege never give up that privilege willingly, and the social institutions that mold our behavior have little incentive to attack that privilege, since their power is tied to population growth.

Burden of proof

The issue of the burden of proof is never explicitly

invoked in discussions about antinatalism, in my experience, but it always lurks in their shadows. People who argue against antinatalism seem to routinely assume that the antinatalist has the burden of proof, and that if the burden is not met (in their eyes, anyway), then some form of natalism must be true. So you have the following classification:

(1) Procreation is wrong.
(2) Procreation is not always wrong.

Now you might think, one of these two must be true, and if (1) is not true then (2) must be true. That's right, but the fact that any given antinatalist fails to prove (1) does not prove that (2) must be true. It is entirely possible that the antinatalist simply didn't give the strongest possible account of their position, perhaps because they are not persuasive enough or because that was not their intention anyway.

But most importantly, the burden of proof does not only apply to (1), but it also applies to (2). Granted, most people assume the burden of proof lies on unpopular positions. I think that this is because we are constantly exposed to popular positions and we naturally assume that it must have evidence backing it up. We rarely think of any popular position as having a burden of proof to meet.

One debate where the burden of proof is constantly raised is the one between theism and atheism. In that case, what we have is the following:

Theism: There is a god.[23]
Atheism: I do not believe that there is a god.

You will notice one major difference between the procreation debate and the god debate: in the latter, there is only one claim about reality, and that's the theistic one. Atheism is not a claim about reality but a personal absence of belief. Some atheists believe there is no god, some don't, but what they all have in common is that they don't believe there is one.

In this debate, the burden of proof is clear: theists have to prove that their position is the correct one. Why? Because otherwise the atheists will simply keep not believing. The atheists, on the other hand, have nothing to demonstrate to the theists, because the atheistic position is purely personal. It does not state that everyone should lack belief in a god, only that the person in question lacks belief in a god.

This is difficult for theists to accept, because they see their position as being the most common one. Why should they have to prove anything? But it is a basic principle of debate that anyone who makes a claim about reality must back it up. In practice, we don't ask for evidence for any claim, only the ones under dispute (in this case, the claim that a god exists), otherwise debates would degenerate into endless chains of proof (can you prove that the Earth is round? can you prove you're not hallucinating right now? and so on and so forth).

In the procreation debate, there are two claims about reality, which I have noted as (1) and (2) above. Both these claims are subject to the burden of proof.

This means two things. First, it means that any failure on the part of any particular debater does not imply the truth of the opposing view. If an antinatalist fails to convince a natalist of the truth of their position, then the natalist cannot claim victory, because their position also has a burden of proof. There is no equivalent to atheism, no lack of belief, but if there was, then it would have to deny belief in both positions:

(3) I do not believe that procreation is wrong, or that it is not always wrong.

Or to say it more simply: "I am not convinced by either side." A person holding to (3) must logically continue to hold that position after being unconvinced by a specific argument, because they will simply keep not believing.

Second, it means that natalists cannot arbitrary exclude themselves from meeting the burden of proof by saying that antinatalism is too outlandish to deserve a response. While I do not deny that antinatalism probably does appear bizarre to many people, this does not in itself prove the truth of natalism. Refuting antinatalist arguments does not prove the truth of natalism, either. To meet the burden of proof, one must present evidence or arguments that demonstrate the truth of a position.

To be clear, even if all the antinatalist arguments

I've discussed in this book were found to be completely faulty, the natalist case would not thereby have been made. One would have to, at best, hold to position (3) until evidence or arguments for natalism were presented. I have presented the main arguments for natalism in chapter 1 and found them severely lacking. In my opinion, no serious case for natalism has yet to be made, and it is unlikely that such a case will ever be made, because that would require natalists to abandon their ultra-simplistic version of the world, where population growth is only a number with no connection to the lives, desires, and suffering of real people. It has the allure that all abstract models have: to paraphrase H. L. Mencken, they reduce extremely complex real life situations to a solution that is clear, simple, and wrong.

Chapter 7
The pro-abortion position

The false dilemma

We have been sold on a certain specific framework on the abortion issue, which segragates the debate into two general positions:

Anti-abortion ("pro-life"): For any given pregnancy, childbirth should be the default (and, by extension, that abortion should be the exception, although some "pro-life" people believe there are no such exceptions).

Pro-choice: For any given pregnancy, freedom for the woman to "choose" between childbirth and abortion should be the default (again, with some exceptions).

These are not mutually exclusive, but rather define a spectrum of personal positions, which differ on issues such as the nature of the situations where abortion should be permitted, and the time limit in weeks when abortion should go from "legal" to "illegal," amongst others.

I want to note that, despite the way it is hammered upon us by both sides in a completely ahistorical way, this framework has not been the norm in Western societies. Rather, legal attacks against abortion have always been part of a package deal,

259

along with attacks against homosexuality, sodomy, and contraception, designed to wrestle control over procreation away from women and forcing them to bear more children in times of demographic crisis. The 14th century saw such attacks in Europe as a consequence of the Black Plague. Another population crisis in the 17th century gave rise to more attacks. The transition to a capitalist economy, which required women to take on the unpaid or low-paid labor of having children, and caring for children (theirs and those of the rich), led to another wave of attacks against abortion, which started with the witch-hunts and ended in the 19th century.[24]

The fight against abortion in the Western world has now become intimately associated with Christian dogma. This association is a relatively recent invention, which is not reflected in the Bible. For most of its existence, the Catholic Church considered abortion to be a non-criminal sin, as long as the fetus was not animated.

This particular framework, and the arguments associated with it, are the product of a wave of attacks which is less than 200 years old. They are not, by far, a universal norm, and the assumption of their universality should be questioned. What is universal is the fact that abortion has always been part of procreative ethics, and all attempts to gain control over procreation must necessarily include abortion.

This is why the antinatalist/childist view on abortion is of relevance here. These positions give us a unique view on the abortion issue. Childism entails that no one should have children unless they are ready to provide the best possible standard of health and care to those children. Antinatalism entails that not having children should be the default position.

These two positions are therefore not part of the standard anti-abortion/pro-choice framework, because they do not promote childbirth or women's "choice." Rather, they promote a third option, which I call pro-abortion, which holds that:

For any given pregnancy, abortion should be the default (and, by extension, that childbirth should be the exception).

Because this option lies wholly outside of the existing framework, it may seem simply unthinkable, or at least absurd on the face of it. After all, gatekeepers for the pro-choice lobby, in attempts to shut down more extreme views as gatekeepers always do, have told us again and again, ad nauseam, that "no one is for abortion." They spend a lot of energy in debates arguing that they don't want abortions any more than the anti-abortion lobby. So if there's one thing that people take away from these debates, it's that any pro-abortion position, like the one I am discussing here, is absolutely impossible.

There is nothing illogical about a pro-abortion position, though. In fact, such a position inscribes itself well within the spectrum that already exists:

people can believe that abortion should be mandated in some situations (such as cases where it is known that the child will be born with some debilitating disease or deformity) and that it should be left to "choice" in other situations, or that abortion should have no time limits in certain situations (as it is in Canada for all pregnancies), and have a time limit in other situations.

It may seem that my anti-childism position contradicts a pro-abortion stance. If children are so important, then why promote a stance that ensures there will be fewer of them? But it is precisely because they devalue children's needs and desires that natalists are able to promote making more of them. Anyone who cares about children should also naturally want fewer children, because the more children there are, the more likely it is that they will be neglected (and that's not counting the millions of children who need homes and who are already being neglected by society). This is why I have been very specific in associating awareness of childism with a deep skepticism towards natalist premises.

Sometimes the pro-choice position is called "pro-abortion," so I must make clear that the pro-abortion stance I am discussing here is not an outgrowth of the pro-choice position at all. I intend to show, amongst other things, that the pro-choice arguments are invalid and are not a good basis on which to develop a position on abortion at all.

The similarities between the pro-choice and anti-

abortion positions

Because this debate has been polarized as a pro-choice versus anti-abortion debate, posing as two opposite sides, it is in their interests to make their position appear to be as distant as possible, to emphasize their differences, to create differences if necessary. So it's important to remember that, as much as they try to look different, the two positions have many important similarities.

1. They believe abortions are undesirable.

Abortions are as desirable as any other surgical operation. Sure, no one likes to have to get surgery, but people who get cancer or atherosclerosis (for example) are likely to desire surgery very much, compared to dying. Likewise, I imagine any given woman would rather not have to get an abortion, but when faced with a pregnancy I have no doubt that a lot of women find an abortion a desirable prospect compared to having a child.

The "abortion is undesirable and we need fewer of them" rhetoric ultimately delivers a natalist message, in that it aims to make women feel that they can't control their own procreative abilities. Both the pro-choice and the anti-abortion positions are inscribed within the war against women, as its moderate and extreme wings.

We see this most notably in the rhetoric used by anti-abortion politicians and activists, who depict women who get abortions as lusty, irresponsible, and unruly, in accordance with the adolescent stereotype model, one of the models which are used to objectify oppressed groups (as discussed in chapter 3). The pro-choice position, while not busy stereotyping women outright, uses the same "choice" rhetoric routinely used by anti-feminists to blame women for their actions under the Patriarchy (I will explain this point later in the chapter).

2. They believe that contraception or abstinence will solve everything.

Pro-choice advocates spread the belief that, if only contraception was widely used, we wouldn't need abortion at all, therefore we must only promote contraception. Anti-abortion advocates, on the other hand, try to spread the idea that contraception doesn't work at all and that abstinence is the only good solution.

Both these beliefs are lies with no connection to the actual data. Contraception does work, and the anti-abortion advocates are simply lying about that, but it's not the magical failproof method that pro-choice advocates pretend it is. Even the most effective contraception methods used in a perfect manner (I am excluding surgical operations like vasectomies here) still yield a 2-6% unintended pregnancy rate per year. This means that over a period of five years, you have an average from 10% to 27% probability of experiencing an unintended pregnancy, again if the contraceptive is used in a perfect manner. Typical (non-perfect) condom use see an approximately 60% probability of unintended pregnancy over five years. This is a gigantic risk to take without abortions being widely available to all. Even vasectomies, done perfectly, yield a 0.5% accidental pregnancies rate over five years.

While these are major problems, abstinence is not a valid solution either. It's simply unrealistic to believe that people will just give up having sex, especially since we indoctrinate boys to believe that being a virgin is shameful and that having sex with a woman is the most important thing they can do to prove their manhood. The regressive and violent religious worldview promoted by the same people who support abstinence has a lot to do with that.

While we need to promote and provide access to contraception, it is not a solution to unintended pregnancies, especially since people's blind faith in contraception, which is a result of pro-choice propaganda, is one of the main causes of unintended pregnancies. Abortion, on the other hand, is a necessary part of the solution: it cannot, in any way, cause unintended pregnancies, and can certainly end them.

3. They are both responsibility-free passes for negligent parents.

In what is by far the most disgusting similarity, pro-choice and anti-abortion advocates share the fact that their positions are both a denial of responsibility towards defective births and children suffering from bad health. No one is responsible for them, it's "God's will" that they be born that way, or it's just "a natural event" and "that's how it is," as if the suffering child popped into existence by magic.

This view is absolutely abhorrent. Even if parents are not aware that their child will be born defective or suffering, they are still very well aware that there is always a chance of any child, including their own, to be born defective or suffering. If you plan an action that has a known risk of harming someone else, and you still do it, you should be held responsible for putting people at risk, and if someone does end up harmed, you should be dealt with. This is just basic justice.

Of course, neither position will ever be willing to acknowledge this basic fact, because they vitally depends on procreation being inherently desirable. To acknowledge that bringing a suffering child into this world is a crime would require them to abandon that fantasy.

4. They ignore the pregnant woman's viewpoint and the child's viewpoint.

At least this is a common criticism addressed to pro-choice and anti-abortion advocates. I am not quite sure to what extent this is really true, but it does seem to be at least somewhat justified; this is especially true in the anti-abortion camp, insofar as they refuse to recognize the morality of abortion altogether, an attitude which by definition requires you to ignore real life.

However, there is one similarity I can definitely point out: the fact that both positions ignore the children's needs. This is also an extension of the previous point, as pushing parental irresponsibility is one of the symptoms of this similarity. In their debates, only the rights and well-being of the fetus is considered relevant, not the rights or well-being of the future child.

One may reply, doesn't the fact that both sides consider possible child deformity as a legalization factor go against my stated similarity? Not really. The formulation of laws revolves around "severe" or "extreme" deformity. To assume that suck laws demonstrate a concern for children is hasty; it could equally demonstrate a concern for the parents' psychological well-being, or a concern against wasteful health care spending (the latter is the most realistic explanation).

Another proof that neither position cares about children is their extremely cavalier treatment of the adoption issue. There is the implicit assumption that the adoption process has no negative effects on the child. People who are aware of the profound trauma of adoption on children, on the other hand, would not promote adoption quite so easily.

5. Both use extreme narratives in their rhetoric on abortion.

The standard anti-abortion narrative is that of "abortion on demand" and "partial-birth abortions," things which are relatively rare. Likewise, they fantasize about doctors cutting babies' heads off and throwing them in the garbage, things of that nature, much like the past prejudices against Jews for killing Christian children and using their blood (the connection between the anti-abortion rhetoric and attitude against abortion doctors, and the rhetoric and attitude of Christians against Jews in past centuries, is hard to miss).

Likewise, the standard pro-choice narrative is based on pregnancies due to rape, again a relatively rare occurrence (approximately 1% of all abortions are due to rape). I am not saying that we should refuse to take such pregnancies into consideration; obviously we should, but this is not a representative narrative for us to think about abortion as an issue.

Both positions use the more extreme examples to typify abortion. These narratives then inform people's political beliefs, and reinforce the ideological gulf between anti-abortion and pro-choice advocates.

What would be a representative narrative? For one thing, the fact that half of pregnancies are unwanted or ambiguous, but that women are too indoctrinated against abortion to even consider having an abortion. This massive fear and repulsion associated with abortion dwarfs the other two narratives by at least two orders of magnitude. So the shift that is necessary here is to go from "this is why women have abortions" to "this is why women do not have abortions." And the culprit is the fear and the shame that both sides put upon pregnant women.

There are three times more children born than there are abortions in a year. This means that there are, roughly, three times more women who refuse to abort (for whatever reason) than women who abort. Instead of assuming that the former is "normal" and that it is the latter that demands explanation, I think we could equally demand an explanation on why women decide to have children instead of aborting, especially given the fact that half of pregnancies are unwanted or ambiguous.

Most of the rest of this chapter will consist of refutations of the main arguments from the pro-choice and the anti-abortion positions. For the anti-abortion side, I will analyze the argument that abortion is murder, as well as the concept of a fetal right to life. For the pro-choice side, I will analyze the self-ownership argument ("my body my choice") and the right to make medical decisions. One argument I will not analyze from the pro-choice side is the "right to procreate," since I've already debunked it in chapter 4.

Abortion is murder

The most used argument by the anti-abortion protesters is that abortion is murder. However, the main problem of this argument revolves around the following issue: murder of what? In normal cases of murder, we can observe that a human being has been killed. But fetuses are not human beings.

Anti-abortion advocates contest that point, and claim that abortion is the murder of an innocent human being. But the very concept of "human being" implies physical independence. A fetus does not, and cannot, live independently from the woman's body, and therefore is not a human being. It does have human DNA, but so does a tumor. Tumors are not human beings either.

Anti-abortion advocates make a big deal out of the fact that a fetus' DNA is a combination of two other humans' DNA. But why does that matter? If a tumor had DNA from two different people, instead of just one, that still would not make it a human being.

This argument becomes even less logical when you consider that most anti-abortion advocates also support exceptions for rape, incest, or risk to the woman's life. But if abortion is murder, this implies that a crime as grave as murder can be magically made non-criminal by another crime. To claim that it is okay to kill someone because one was the victim of rape or incest, when that someone had nothing to do with the rape or incest, is profoundly illogical and demonstrates how they don't take "abortion is murder" seriously at all.

According to the 2006 iteration of the General Social Survey, 70% of American anti-abortion advocates also believe in the death penalty, which makes the "abortion is murder" argument all the more puzzling. If most of them just don't care about murdering innocent human beings (as you must if you believe in the death penalty), then what does it matter if abortion is the murder of innocent human beings anyway?

I also want to point out that the objections used by pro-choice people are almost as bad. For instance, one common reply is that, whether abortion is murder or not, women will keep doing it anyway, and so there's no point in making abortion illegal. But one can say that about any crime. Should we make rape legal because men will keep raping either way? Should we make fraud legal because scammers will exist whether it's legal or not? Surely we could make rape and fraud "safer" for their victims if it was legal? Such a reasoning should disgust anyone.

Another reply is that abortion, when done early enough, cannot be murder because all it does is remove the fetus from the womb. The woman "simply" stops providing resources to the fetus.

But this is a disingenuous argument, as everyone knows that the fetus will die if it is deprived of the woman's bodily resources. Likewise, if you stop feeding a baby, it will also die. Does that mean we should be able to starve babies to death without consequence? Does that mean we should pull the cords off of people in comas, or stop feeding invalids? This is basically an argument for torture, not for abortion.

Incidentally, this view of abortion politics is grounded in the concept that there is no such thing as "positive rights" (i.e. that we have no obligation to provide anything to anyone), which is associated with right-wing types, anti-welfare, anti-health care types, people who tend to be anti-abortion. This is not a view that most liberals hold to. Why they would suddenly become strict right-wingers when the issue of fetuses comes up, I have no idea.

This cruel line of reasoning reflects the general pro-choice rhetoric that the fetus is the legal equivalent of a home invader, and that we should treat both the same way. But surely associating fetuses with human beings who have evil intentions cannot have any good consequences. While fetuses are not human beings, it seems pointless to degrade them in this way when we already have a perfectly meaningful response to the argument anyway.

Fetal right to life

Another argument commonly presented by anti-abortion advocates is that fetuses have the right to life, and that they are speaking up for the fetus' interests. If fetuses have a right to life, then we shouldn't let other people try to kill them until said fetuses grow up and become able to speak for themselves.

Only human beings have rights. That being said, we recognize that some actions taken against a fetus go against the rights of the future person (i.e. the child that will develop from that fetal stage). For instance, we happen to think that pregnant women shouldn't smoke, drink, or take drugs. These things are mostly legal, but the possibility of having laws regulating the behavior of pregnant women to protect the health of children is regularly brought up. If we accept the belief that children are human beings and that human beings have a right to health, then it seems reasonable to say that there are fetal rights not to be subjected to tobacco, alcohol or other drugs.

But is there a fetal right to life? I contend that such a right is logically impossible. For the fetus embodies rights only insofar as the fetus will develop into a child which does have rights. We see a pregnant woman drinking or smoking as unethical because the future child will lose its access to the highest quality of health possible. But when a fetus is aborted, the connection between that fetus and the future child is severed. Therefore we cannot say that the fetus has a right to life.

Just to be clear, I am not saying that the abortion somehow removes the fetus' rights. If that was what I was saying, then a critic could argue that one could apply the same reasoning to actual murder, that killing someone removes their rights and that therefore murder is not really wrong, and therefore prove my position invalid ad absurdum.

No, what I am saying is that the aborted fetus never embodied any rights at all, for we would see nothing wrong with a pregnant woman drinking or smoking if she was then going to abort the fetus on the next day. The fetus' rights are wholly conditional to its continued existence as a future

273

child. A human being, on the other hand, has unconditional rights which are infringed upon by the act of murder.

The self-ownership argument

The argument most often used by pro-choice advocates can be expressed as "the woman owns her own body, so she decides" (or as some write on their signs, "my body my choice"). According to a commonly quoted pro-choice article on the subject of abortion:

> You cannot have two entities with equal rights occupying one body. One will automatically have veto power over the other – and thus they don't have equal rights. In the case of a pregnant woman, giving a "right to life" to the potential person in the womb automatically cancels out the mother's right to Life, Liberty, and the Pursuit of Happiness.
>
> After birth, on the other hand, the potential person no longer occupies the same body as the mother, and thus, giving it full human rights causes no interference with another's right to control her body.

But this is clearly nonsense, for the same reason I discussed in the previous section: babies are just as dependent on the mother's body as fetuses, merely in a different way. Having a baby definitely does "cause interference" with the mother's right to control her body. Therefore the attempt at making a distinction between before birth and after birth is invalid, and so is the argument.

Now, granted, the baby does not occupy the same body as the mother, while the fetus does, but this doesn't serve any role in the argument, since it does not get us any closer to the conclusion that the rights of the fetus cancel out the mother's rights.

To come back to the main argument, self-ownership is incoherent. One cannot be said to own one's body, because the concept of ownership implies a relation between owner and owned. For example, when we say "I own this table" we are expressing a relation between me (owner) and table (owned) mediated by society (property rights). Saying "I own my body" is meaningless because I am my body.

Society at large does not recognize self-ownership, either. While our concept of ownership includes buying and selling owned objects, we do not, by and large, recognize a right for individuals to sell themselves into slavery or to buy other people.

I don't think that people really mean it when they make claims of self-ownership. I think "my body" merely refers to a statement about women being free to decide what they want to do. But if that's the case, then "my body my choice" becomes a tautology: "I am free to decide, therefore I am free to decide." Like all tautologies, it is ultimately

275

meaningless and can prove nothing.

Now, are women (or any human being, for that matter) "free to decide" anything? To assume so means assuming the issue at hand, whether abortion should be left to a personal decision. In general, we acknowledge that there are severe limits to people's freedom of action, especially when other people are involved. Either way, the argument needs to be proven, and I will refute one such attempt at a proof in the next section.

The right to make medical decisions

Should people have the right to make medical decisions about their own bodies? At first glance, this question seems like a no-brainer. Surely people should be free to approve or reject any medical operation performed on their own bodies.

However, when the well-being of other people is involved, the situation becomes far less clear-cut. Mandatory vaccinations serve the common good, and without them more people (especially children) are at risk of getting debilitating or fatal diseases. In that regard, mandatory vaccinations are similar to gun control or preventing drunk driving: no one has the right to impose a perilous or fatal risk on others, and we should prevent that from happening, by force if necessary. People should not be able to choose whether to get vaccinated or not (or whether "their children" get vaccinated or not).

Likewise, we don't allow people traveling with a dangerous infectious disease to decide whether they should be put in quarantine or not. Again, people's medical freedom must be limited by the gravity of the risk they are imposing on other people. The greater the risk, the more imposition we should allow. No one should be quarantined for having a cold, but we expect people to be quarantined if they have, say, the ebola virus.

Every single pregnancy is a heavy health risk imposed on another human being- the future person. All new people, at birth, face a risk of debilitating deformity or disease equivalent to, or greater than, the risks we protect ourselves from by vaccinations or quarantine. So positing a right for women to make medical decisions about pregnancies is the equivalent of positing a right for people to decide whether they should be quarantined or whether they should be vaccinated: it first requires one to ignore the fact that it coerces other people to be subjected to heavy (and potentially fatal) risks. There cannot be a human right that coerces others to face such risks.

The anti-abortion contingent has its own argument under this category, pertaining to the medical providers: they argue that providers should have the right to refuse to perform medical procedures, or refuse to provide medications, if they object to those procedures or medications. But this is no more logical than the pro-choice argument: medical providers can have no more "right" to put people at risk by refusing to provide medical services than people can have the "right" to put people at risk by refusing to get vaccinated or quarantined.

They say it has to do with "following your conscience." But this is about bigotry, not conscience: we should no more allow shopkeepers to ban black people from their establishment than we should allow doctors to refuse to serve pregnant women's needs. If your conscience tells you that abortion and abortion-related medications are wrong, then maybe you shouldn't be in a position to have to deliver them in the first place. Being a pharmacist or a doctor and being against abortions is kinda like being a politician and being against dishonesty: something doesn't add up.

Choice-talk is misogynist talk

The concept of choice, and its academic big brother, the concept of agency, superficially appear to be nice terms that everyone can get behind. Isn't it good that we have choice and can decide for ourselves? Shouldn't we grant agency to people, instead of pretending that they are powerless? Shouldn't we stop treating people like victims, and instead tell them that they're empowered to take their lives into their own hands?

Unfortunately, I've found that, when these concepts are used in a political setting (such as that of abortion), they are almost uniformly used to blame the victim. We are told that calling people who were raped "victims" denies their agency, because they were partially responsible for what happened to them. We are told that prostituted women (who are at heavy risk of getting killed and raped) chose to do what they do, and that excuses every risk they face. We are told by the pro-choice side that abortion is a regrettable choice, and that we must persuade people to choose contraception instead of abortions.

In all these cases, the concepts of choice and agency are used as a stand-in for "it's really their fault." In the case that interests us, abortion, it is implied that it's women's fault for not using contraception, or not getting the man to use contraception. What if the woman doesn't have access to contraception? What if she did use contraception, and it failed (as will inevitably happen to many millions of women every year)? What if she was intimidated or coerced into having sex without contraception? What if a defect is detected in the fetus? Implicitly, we are supposed to conclude that she is always to blame for getting an abortion. The anti-abortion stereotype of the promiscuous single woman who collects abortions is only an extension of this premise.

Choice and agency are terms used to hide the real reasons why women get into these situations. Talking about the agency of rape victims obfuscates the fact that someone (almost always, a man) coerced them in some way into sex. Talking about the choice that prostituted women made obfuscates the fact that most of them resort to prostitution out of sexual alienation and/or poverty, and that the vast majority of them want to leave. Talking about the regrettable choice of abortion omits the fact that all the reasons I've given are beyond a woman's control, and are not her fault. In most cases, abortion is not regrettable, it's a fact of life.

By putting their emphasis on women's choice to abort, while at the same time devaluing abortions, the pro-choice position ironically degenerates into the same sort of misogyny used by right-wingers to justify the exploitation of women. The pro-choice position, however, is more desirable, in the sense that leaving it to women's choice is far better to coercing all women to bring their pregnancies to term. While pro-choice arguments are no more right than anti-abortion arguments, the pro-choice can be said to be "less wrong," if there is such a thing, because at least they take into account the needs of women.

However, they still do not take into account the needs of children. They prop up only one leg of my argument. We cannot make a correct evaluation of the control over procreation without taking into account the rights and interests of both women and children.

"You can't choose for someone else!"

Since the pro-choice position is centered around the "freedom to choose," there is no doubt in my mind that the pro-choice reply to the pro-abortion position would be similar to their reply to the anti-abortion position: "You can't choose for pregnant women!"

This statement is trivially true, in the sense that no one can think for anyone else. But as I already mentioned, I think that when pro-choice advocates talk about "ownership" or "choice" they are really just making an exaggerated claim to freedom.

But there are always limits to freedom. No society has ever existed that permitted its own people to make their own choices as regards to murder, theft, rape, or assault. We "choose for" everyone that they should not do any of these things, or at least not do them in ways that are not permitted. If this is the standard of freedom, then no free society can exist, because no society could survive for long if people did not have a basic fundamental respect of each other. So this conception of freedom is necessarily nihilistic.

We generally recognize that human beings have rights (or whatever other moral construct you wish to use as a substitute). And one of the most fundamental rights, I contend, is the right of children to the highest possible standard of health. Without good health, any of the supposed rights we have as adults become meaningless, empty phrases. Therefore, if my view is correct, pregnant women should not have the freedom to give birth to a compromised child, or potentially compromised child.

But we can also turn this argument around. The person who supports the freedom to bring pregnancies to term is also choosing for someone else: the future person. They are implicitly stating that the condition of this world is good enough to bring a new person into it, otherwise they wouldn't support doing so. But this is a personal preference, not a fact.

They are most definitely "choosing for someone else," a choice which they simply assume the future person would agree with. But any assumption that the future person will enjoy their life (based on dubious statistics) does not justify choosing for that person. Also consider that giving birth is followed by 18 years of child-raising which in itself implies a great deal of constant "choosing for someone else." If it's wrong to choose for pregnant women, then it is doubly wrong to choose for future persons, and force them to experience the repercussions of that choice.

Childbirth is a violent act

In my examination of the pro-abortion on my blog, I asked commenters to answer one of two questions, depending on their professed position:

> (anti-abortion) What maximum number of women dead from botched back alley abortions per year do you consider a fair and just tradeoff to prevent all abortions that would happen under a pro-abortion scheme?
>
> (pro-choice) What maximum number of children afflicted with spina bifita/Tay-

282

> Sachs/leukemia/cancer/Downs Syndrome/etc a year do you consider a fair and just tradeoff to prevent the distress of women who would not be allowed to have a child under a pro-abortion scheme?

It shouldn't be too surprising that no one was ready to provide an answer. No one likes to be cornered with such uncomfortable questions. To give an actual number would mean portraying themselves as violent tormentors instead of victims, which means they would lose their moral high ground. Anti-abortion people cannot acknowledge their responsibility for back alley abortions because that would expose their profound misogyny. Pro-choice people cannot acknowledge their responsibility for birth defects because that would expose their profound childism (but since childism is mostly acceptable in our societies anyway, I doubt they actually have much to fear from that).

But when those same people argue against antinatalism, you hear a different story. Then they argue that suffering is a necessary part of life, and that therefore we should just accept things like back alley abortions or child leukemia (even though the more logical conclusion should be to reject life as an ethical positive). Of course, they still won't give numbers, but the fact remains that their positions entail doing violence against someone.

Now, I freely admit that the same is true of the pro-abortion position. While I think that the pro-abortion position entails vastly less suffering than the alternatives, it still involves coercing people, just as the pro-choice and anti-abortion positions do. My intent has not been to make a utilitarian argument, but rather to demonstrate that the opposing arguments are very weak, far weaker, at least in my view, than the arguments (anti-childism and antinatalism) supporting the pro-abortion position.

Childbirth is violent not only in its repercussions, but also in itself. As de Giraud writes:

> To see a recent birth, his body creased, cyanotic, asphyxiated, as the medical literature admits, to contemplate his face labored with cries, his eyes lashed with anxiety, his cheeks raked by tears, who would doubt that he just went through the equivalent of a beatdown by a horde of cavemen? What sadism for parents to inflict, in full knowledge of the cause, such mistreatment, such hardships, on their "dearest"?
>
> Specialty books... readily invoke the "state of shock" in which the newborn finds itself and can only recommend a caesarian delivery when fetal distress becomes extreme (i.e. when the agony felt by the baby pushes it closer and closer to death, pure and simple); in a most serious fashion, some even risk to compare the fetus' violent passage from a protective aqueous medium to a hostile aerial environment with the

hardships experienced by an astronaut deprived of his spacesuit!

And is there any doubt in anyone's mind that babies are in a state of constant discomfort? Babies cry for all sorts of reasons: because they are hungry, soiled, gassy, teething, cold, hot, or even because they got their circulation cut off by something as tiny as a hair. The life of a baby is as agonizing as its birth. We are so desensitized to this painful existence that we treat a baby crying as a commonplace occurrence.

Of course I am not saying that we should treat the suffering of a baby being born or crying as the end of the world, otherwise we should never get anything done; but we should curse and spit on the parents who brought it into the world to feel that pain in the first place, and try to limit that suffering as much as humanly possible by reducing the number of new lives.

I hope you'll excuse me if I briefly get theological. I certainly don't believe in the myth of Eden, but there is a fruitful comparison to be made here. It tells of a garden where everything was provided to the first humans, where they did not have to toil or experience suffering. But once they are deceived into taking in knowledge of good and evil, they are kicked out of Eden and forced to live in the outside world, where they have to toil and experience constant suffering. Especially interesting is the fact that childbirth, which is sold to us as a great life experience, is given to humans by God as a *punishment*! On that count, at least, the Bible knows where it's at.

But there is not my main point. Rather, I want to compare the Eden story with childbirth. In the womb, the fetus is fed without any effort on its part. It does not suffer at all, as fetuses do not experience physical pain and they are not developed enough to feel psychological pain. Not only that, but it is innocent, unaware of even the existence of pain.

Childbirth represents a great trauma: the fetus is forcibly ejected from the womb, into the outside world, where suffering exists and where nourishment is no longer provided automatically. The new baby is now keenly aware of the existence of pain, and will be for the rest of its life. It will have to toil for its nourishment, at first by experiencing hunger and waiting for its food, and later to actually work for money to buy food.

I think I've made the analogy obvious enough. The womb is our own personal Eden, where everything was provided for us, where we did not, and could not, suffer. Childbirth is the Fall of man(kind), more specifically, of every single human being that exists. It is literally a disaster of Biblical proportions.

There are all sorts of interpretations as to what the Garden of Eden story is supposed to tell us. Some believe that it is a story about the "soul" (whatever that is) entering the human body. Others believe it is about maturing and going into the world as adults. I find the second interpretation interesting because it heavily relies on two points: the knowledge of good and evil, and the capacity to procreate, which are both seen as signs of maturity.

The former goes against everything we know in moral development, as we know that children, even babies, have a sense of morality. But to equate procreation with maturity is particularly egregious. This is the result of prejudice against childfree women, who are called immature and selfish because they do not have children. But, again, giving birth is not portrayed as a sign of maturity but as a punishment etched in pain. It is something to be feared, not something to be cherished.

It is commonly said that right-wingers love fetuses but hate them once they're born by refusing to provide parents with the services that they need to raise their children. I deny the first part of that sentiment. Being in favor of forced childbirth is not love, not for children or for anyone else; it means to deliberately start a new person's life with torture and pain. It is not a contradiction to be anti-abortion and to be anti-welfare. Both manifest a profound hatred of one's own humanity.

Chapter 8
The social effects of childism

There are almost two billion children in the world. Everyone has once been a child and been raised by some adults (generally by one's parents) in a pedagogical manner. These two facts mean that childism, like sexism and racism, has profound repercussions on the world.

Unlike the victims of gender or race discrimination, children most often need the support and help of adults to have safe spaces and to grasp their existence as a class, and most adults are against granting them either of those things. But there are many similarities between the effects of sexism and racism on society and the effects of childism on society.

1. Childism provides the justification for innumerable immoral or criminal acts (verbal and physical violence, incest, forced labor, coercion).

All around the world, the inferior social and legal status of children is used as a justification for acts which would be illegal if committed against adults. And most of these acts do not have any value in terms of child development: most of the time they obviously serve the interests and the ego of the parents or other authority figures. A child getting spanked or beaten, demeaned, raped, coerced to work for a family concern without pay, is the victim of an immoral or criminal act which serves the parents' interests, not their interests. Parents act in these ways for sexual gratification, to boost their ego, to cow their children into obedience, for money, for status.

Whether parents like it or not, the only frameworks that help us understand why these crimes have been, and are being, committed are the frameworks of objectification and ownership. The child is seen, not as a human being with needs and values, but as an emotional, sexual and labor resource. This resource is under the control of the family, which can dictate how it's used. After all, the child should not have any say about its life, as it is undeveloped, devoid of good judgment, and cannot possibly know what's best for itself.

The child is not just a resource for its parents but also for social institutions, which see children as a future reproductive, financial or labor resource. This mentality underlies things like the forced enrollment of children in public schools and the "stay in school" mentality, the neurotypical bigotry manifested in the drugging of children, and the religious promotion of strict gender roles. These attitudes are reflected in the way parents indoctrinate their children to become breeders and successful workers.

Childism also makes children more vulnerable to further abuse. As reflected in our pedagogies, it demands that children respect authority figures (know their proper place in the hierarchy) and implies that love is expressed by punishment as well as affection (love is control). Both these precepts make children more vulnerable to abuse from other authority figures, and even strangers. Furthermore, abusers often use the child's family as emotional blackmail against the child revealing the abuse ("if you tell anyone, I'll kill your parents!"), which entraps children in repeated abuse.

Genderism, racism and other prejudices intersect with childism to compound the violence done to children. One cannot overstate the intellectual stunting of girls, the persecution of girls, and gynocides, committed around the world. One cannot overstate the child slavery and human trafficking, for which imperialism is in no small part responsible, being perpetrated around the world.

Although less harmful in themselves, but not to be neglected in any examination of the crimes committed against children, children's stories have traditionally served the role of threatening punishment to children for failing to obey[25]: threatening children with death, kidnapping or beatings is a criminal act. We do not consider these threats criminal because we consider narratives to be silly things on the whole, only important at all if they qualify as "art." Otherwise they are just harmless, edifying stories for children. Fortunately, we seem to have left these kinds of narratives behind, and seem to mostly reserve the abusive stories for teenage girls (as the Twilight series famously showed).

Perhaps the most threatening narrative of them all is

the threat of Hell. To children who have been indoctrinated into Christianity and the belief in Heaven and Hell, there is probably nothing scarier than the prospect of going to Hell for being disobedient, and that can leave psychological scars for the rest of your life. More than half of the people of the world believe in some kind of eternal damnation and suffering. That's a lot of children being indoctrinated to believe that their eternal fate depends on their religious affiliation and obedience.

Some have tried to justify this indoctrination by saying that belief in Hell lower crime rates. But this is the same kind of argument used to justify spanking and other forms of assault against children. The goal is to scar the child psychologically so much that they internalize the fear of authority (the parents, and then the school, the laws, the church, and so on) and fear breaking their rules. There is nothing good in that, there is no happiness to be found in living like this, there is no place for a child's moral compass to develop in a healthy and rational manner. It is child abuse in the name of law and order.

2. Childism provides the justification for the complete control that parents exert over a child's life.

Regimented parental control over a child's existence in time and space (and by extension the same control exerted by schools) is justified by the child's supposed lack of judgment. Children don't know what's best for their development, so parents (and other authority figures) must decide for them what activities they should be occupied with, the spaces they should use to do so, and how they should use those spaces. Generally, this control is not exercised arbitrarily or capriciously, and no parent thinks they give such orders arbitrarily, despite the fact that they generally have no experience or expertise in the area of child development.

As I've pointed out before, most parents are not qualified to raise children, based on the standards we impose on actual, educated child care workers. In practice, parents usually either use the same methods of child-raising used on them as children, or they fall back to the latest pedagogical fad (which always have cutesy, unscientific names like "helicopter parenting," "tiger parenting" or "dolphin parenting"). So the belief that parents are the people most able to make decisions about their children's lives would be laughable, if it wasn't so horrifying.

Since all child-raising methods can only become popular by appealing to parents, not children, they must appeal to the ego of the parents and cannot upset the childist hierarchy. This is why no pedagogy, no matter how well intentioned, can be "on the side of the child." They are all about controlling children in order to bring about desirable outcomes.

One cannot make specific statements about this control because parents vary wildly in their pedagogic styles and families wildly differ in living arrangements. Some children cannot have friends their parents disapprove of, and others can. Some children are very limited in how they can spend their free time and some are not so limited. Some children are "in the system" and bandied from family to family, some are split between two divorced parents, and others are rooted to one home.

But it's not hard to pinpoint the nature of the control: the constant invalidation of the child's beliefs, values, preferences and feelings. If the parents believe that their child should be free to choose something, then they will be, but this does not mean that the child is thereby free. A "right" that can be taken away at any time is a privilege, not a right.

It is part of the nature of the childist hierarchy that children are followers and adults are leaders: the concept of children as leaders simply does not compute to them, and is generally interpreted as "letting children run amok." But as A.S. Neill's Summerhill School has demonstrated, children being given leadership in the areas of their lives that they care about does not lead to disaster, rather the opposite. Like anti-feminists who associate matriarchy with women controlling men, and racists who associate race equality with mob violence, childists associate the idea of children as leaders with children having power over adults. Opposition to equality is justified as fear of role reversal.

3. Childism provides the justification for forcing children to live in ways which hinder their physical, mental and moral development.

This is an extension of point 2, because it is the complete control that parents, and other authority figures, use against children which makes possible the stunting of their development (often done in the name of that same development).

One could talk a great deal about forced labor and child slavery, which are massive worldwide issues (more than 200 million children live under forced labor, for example). These issues are not solely childist and child-hatred issues, but prejudice against children and hatred of children is a part of them. But one must also extend the conversation beyond forced labor and child slavery, to untold generations of children who have had to work for their parents' welfare under parental pressure or intimidation.

Children have one job, and that's being children. Their work is to learn to walk, talk, and write, to play, to figure out how to take their place amongst other children, to figure out what they like. Anything beyond that slows down, or stops, the child's development as a person, and does not serve the interests of the child. Making children work for the benefit of the parents, or anyone else, is a profoundly selfish act.

One can also look at children raised under the shadow of religious sects or cults. They are raised in a harmful environment, subjected to extreme brainwashing, and most of the time remain isolated from mainstream culture, all because they are considered owned by their parents (and since the parents owe allegiance to the cult, it is assumed that the children do as well).

By pure accident of birth, a child may be subjected to brutal or violent parents for its entire childhood. A child may be subjected to verbally abusive or manipulative parents who confuse or psychologically damage it, to the point where that child later becomes a drug addict, suicidal or self-destructive, and so on (but one must not, and cannot, blame the child or the adult it becomes, for the blame falls entirely on the parents). A child may experience a devastating, damaging childhood, and has no recourse against the parents who imposed it.

But even if the parents are well-intentioned, accidents happen. A parent may die or become injured, unable to work or support the child. Jobs can be lost, financial situations can turn bad. Even though this makes little sense logically, as I've discussed earlier, more than one-fifth of American children live in poverty. That is childism.

4. Childism justifies the forced identification imposed on children.

Through the alignment paradigm, children are forcibly indoctrinated to identify with a multitude of social constructs, such as gender, race, religion, nationality and intelligence. Young children (at least those that are too young to go to school) are not social agents, and therefore do not, and cannot, have a gender, a religion or a nationality, since these concepts arise from our social roles (and I would argue that even though it has a physical component, a child should not be given a race identification either). A child should have only one social role: being a child. Anything else is a lie, an unfair and unnecessary burden, and a denial of the child's freedom of thought (and therefore of adults' freedom of thought as well).

According to the paradigm, children must hold the correct beliefs and align their preferences with what's "normal" in their assigned culture in order to ensure that they develop correctly and fit in with the rest of society. The role of the child is not to be a child, but to become (transform into) a good citizen, a good Christian, a masculine man or a feminine woman, college-educated, and so on.

Religion has been especially good at creating a captive audience by brainwashing children, and it's a strategy that works as long as you also heavily promote natalism. Most other constructs are promoted by parents, I think, mostly out of fear or sincere belief: fear that their children will not "come out" right, or sincere belief that their children will be better people if they are correctly indoctrinated.

Strong indoctrination is especially needed in the cases of religion and gender, because both of these constructs entail a certain set of behaviors and beliefs, and many child have a personality which clashes with those behaviors and beliefs. It is therefore necessary to stomp down gender non-conforming children and non-believing children, with all the psychological torture that this implies (blackmail, destruction of the child's self-image, withdrawal of love, and so on).

A further effect of indoctrination is to divide children against each other. They fight for grades, they compete in sports, they berate each other for not performing gender correctly, for being of the "wrong" religion, for not being smart enough or being too smart. Meanwhile, cooperation is institutionally marginalized and devalued in schools. This has the effect of neutralizing any possibility of class consciousness in children.

5. Childism justifies the use of a prejudicial framework that demeans and stereotypes children.

I want to illustrate this point by taking two real-life examples of this prejudicial framework. These are ostensibly studies on child behavior, but they have a clear childist agenda. The first has been featured in many places under the bizarre title "Babies are not as innocent as they pretend":

> Dr Vasudevi Reddy, of the University of Portsmouth's psychology department, says she has identified seven categories of deception used between six months and three-years-old.
>
> Infants quickly learnt that using tactics such as fake crying and pretend laughing could win them attention. By eight months, more

> difficult deceptions became apparent, such as concealing forbidden activities or trying to distract parents' attention.

Wow, children want to get attention and don't want to be punished. An incredible scientific discovery, if you're deeply stupid, but labeling such things as a baby crying, laughing and concealing information "deception" and "deviousness" is absolutely ridiculous. A six month old baby is not "deceiving" its parents any more than it "resists" orders, "pretends" to be innocent, or "seduces" its rapist (as is often argued in the case of child rape).

This is pretty standard bigoted rhetoric retooled for childist purposes. While POC or women may seem "innocent," they are actually "deceptive" and plotting behind your back at all times, very clear expressions of the adolescent model used by racists, sexists, classists, and other assorted bigots. As any of them will tell you, "you can never trust *those* people."

The general principle is that inferiors, those who don't have the control, are not allowed to defend themselves. Those who do are called uppity, crazy, devious or ungrateful. Their needs and feelings are trivialized and negated. A small child, who has no control over its own life and must obtain everything through its parents, has no choice but to manipulate its parents in order to get what it wants. To use this as a proof that babies use "deception" is profoundly offensive.

Another study discusses the amount of cheating done in schools:

> At the Pre-School level children understand that cheating is morally wrong, as opposed to a social transgression (i.e. eating with their fingers). Because moral development consists of their own needs vs. punishment, they are prone to cheat in order to win.
>
> At 5-6 years of age many children cheat if the opportunity arises. In one study of this age group, 84% knew that cheating was not allowed. However, 56% cheated. This is primarily true because they have an inability to inhibit their actions at this age.

I don't have the details of this study, but the writeup is glib at best. As the study was financed by an anti-cheating organization (whose propaganda could provide quite a bit of fodder about authoritarian morality), they have an interest in presenting cheating as morally wrong, and they have an interest in presenting cheating as a widespread problem.

To portray cheating as wrong only makes sense if one holds the "objective" testing of children's abilities as necessary, and only someone with a vested interest in child indoctrination would hold such a belief. Obviously most children know cheating is considered wrong by teachers, but do they "understand" that it's "morally wrong"? I certainly don't think it's morally wrong.

Again, we observe the same principle as in the previous example: with their intelligence and the good will of their parents threatened by bad exam results, children defend themselves by cheating, and this is portrayed as a defect of character. Instead of taking the side of the child, and questioning the perceived necessity of relentless competitive testing, we side against the child and accuse it of being immoral or incapable.

I'm sure many people will accuse me of supporting the actions of bad apples and that surely some children act mendaciously. My answer is that it really does not matter at all, because they all deal with a hostile system in their own way and none of them should be blamed for cheating. The dispossessed should never be blamed for the ways they find to deal with an unjust system.

6. Childism supports and is supported by religious and psychological doctrines such as Original Sin and Freudian psychology, which invalidate children's experiences and demand that they forgive their abusers.

These are topics on which Alice Miller has written extensively. In her book The Untouched Key, she discusses the Biblical story of Isaac and Jacob. She has also written about her days as a psychotherapist and how she discovered that Freudian theories serve to cover up and repress fear and abuse in childhood.

Alice Miller was aware that the constant and

unrelenting demand that children forgive their parents, their abusers, could only beat a person down to complete and abject submission:

> [Some therapists] work under the influence of various interpretations culled from both Western and Oriental religions, which preach forgiveness to the once-mistreated child. Thereby, they create a new vicious circle for people who, from their earliest years, have been caught in the vicious circle of pedagogy. This, they refer to as "therapy". In so doing, they lead them into a trap from which there is no escape, the same trap that once rendered their natural protests impossible, thus causing the illness in the first place. Because such therapists, caught as they are in the pedagogic system, cannot help patients to resolve the consequences of the traumatization they have suffered, they offer them traditional morality instead.

But Miller's main concern was the repetition compulsion, the compulsion on the part of parents to repeat the abuse that was inflicted on them as children. This is all based on the deception perpetrated on them, when their parents made them believe that unconditional love included, or even needed, invalidation, emotional blackmail, control and abuse. No one who was raised to believe this about love can raise their own children with love.

> They are repeating the "sins" of their parents BECAUSE they have forgiven them. If they

301

could consciously condemn the deeds of their parents they wouldn't be urged to do the same, to molest and to confuse children by forcing them to stay silent – as if this was the most normal thing to do and not a crime. They just deceive themselves.

7. Childism justifies our lack of interest in providing for future generations.

A salient fact about our current politics is the lack of interest from our political elites, as well as the general population, in ensuring the well-being and safety of future generations.

Part of the reason is because doing so would mean uprooting major social institutions, like the capitalist system, and this is not something politically viable in most countries. But I think childism is another big reason for that. In a system where there is not even any attempt at representing the interests of future generations, we cannot expect for the outcome to be future-oriented. Capitalism and neo-liberalist politics are all about profit at the expense of people, mortgaging the future of humanity for the sake of present surpluses.

We see this most starkly in issues like overpopulation, global warming, the depletion of resources on this planet, or neo-liberalism wrecking economies and killing people around the world, but we also see it in more local issues. In fact, childism is invoked against local policies: for instance, people who oppose minimum wage raises often say they do so because it only affects children and young adults, and therefore is not worth thinking about (as it happens, the statistics show they're dead wrong, but their prejudice is more important than facts). And I think Americans will be familiar with so-called "abstinence classes," another political issue motivated by childism.

The issue of representation is an important one. Poor people who acquire the resources necessary to gain political influence are no longer classified as poor, which means that poor people will always be underrepresented. Likewise, people who are old enough to participate in political discourse, and have the intellectual awareness and sophistication to see themselves as part of a child class, are also generally too old to be classified as children.

But even if they were represented in the political process, children would still not be taken seriously if they talked about issues concerning children as a class. Because of childism, we believe that children have no values or desires worth talking about, and that their ideas are only worth discussing if they are ideas about adult values or desires.

***

It may seem like I've spent a lot of space here on childism, a subject which is not usually associated with procreative ethics (people who talk about childism at all mostly talk about it from the point of view of being just another prejudice), but I believe that it's a vitally important part of the discussion.

This book is about exploring the other two sides of the procreative triangle, women and children. And without some awareness of childism, there is no reason for anyone to want to look at the children side of the triangle.

Antinatalist arguments imply some awareness of childism, and natalist arguments imply a complete lack of such awareness. After all, natalists will routinely reply to the duty argument by saying that the suffering of children should not concern us (of course they always have some excuse to rationalize this). Only someone who has no concern for children whatsoever would think that inflicting suffering on a new human life is a trivial fact.

As such, childism is most important, I think, as the way to force children's interests into the conversation, like how feminism has succeeded in forcing women's interests into public discourse. Generally speaking, Western cultures no longer see women solely as objects of desire (although clearly they still do), but also as human beings with their own values, desires, and rights. This has had an impact on a great number of political and ethical issues, including the important procreative issue of abortion. I believe that awareness of childism could have a similar impact on many issues, not the least being procreative ethics as they are currently practiced.

Chapter 9
Formulating an alternative to natalism

The aim of this book is to present the two main lines of evidence, childism and antinatalism, which take procreative ethics away from men's economic and social interests and into women's and children's interests. The task of formulating a practical alternative to the prevalent natalist policies is beyond the scope of this book, but, as a conclusion of sorts, I would like to look at some considerations about practicalities.

First of all, I am not optimistic about childism theory or antinatalism ever being adopted as policy, or even becoming part of public discourse. If either of these positions become more widespread, it will be in the long-term and would require a major shift in attitudes towards children and procreation. I don't even want to speculate on how that could happen, as that would be more science-fiction than anything else.

Side issues like childfreedom and abortion are gaining traction, which is encouraging. These positions encourage people who already don't want children to take control over their procreation, but unfortunately they do not prevent or convince those who do want children to not breed. Because those people are the vast majority of us (around 95% of the population in the United States: I was unable to find statistics for other countries), that means that childfreedom and abortion in themselves can only have a marginal (important, but marginal) effect.

So what can be done to alleviate the burden of procreation? One solution which is jokingly invoked in the mainstream is the concept of procreative licenses, the standard joke being "we need a licence to drive, but how come we don't need a licence to have children?" People are not allowed to take the idea seriously because doing so is an attack against our supposed "right to procreate."

In order for the concept of procreative licenses to be taken seriously, it would be necessary for procreation to be reframed as a privilege, like driving, and not a right. Actually, I think you can make a much stronger case for driving being a right, since in most places in the world you do need to drive in order to work, buy food, or otherwise participate in society. Procreation, on the other hand, is a selfish and inconsiderate act, which does not contribute to any person's basic standard of life and is not necessary for any vital activity. Furthermore, existing child care standards demonstrate that most parents are not capable of raising children to any satisfactory level.

Daniel Mackler, who I quoted in chapter 4, has an elaborate proposal for the standards by which these licenses would be granted. Categories in which couples would have to prove their abilities include having a committed and stable relationship, emotional health, physical health, being between 25 and 40 years old, having experience with other people's children, being able to earn a living, being financially stable, and having a college degree.

These criteria may seem harsh, and I don't agree with all of them. But there is no doubt in my mind that we cannot guarantee children's well-being in families which do not meet at least most of these standards. You may argue that these standards are much more strict than the ones we impose on child care workers, but child care workers are not financially responsible for the children they care for, and do not have to form a family bond with them.

It is commonly believed that people who have children all have an innate capacity to raise children in a correct way. Given the percentage of children who are verbally, physically, or sexually abused every year, we know this is not true, by a long shot. Most people (and I include my wife and myself in that statement) should not, under any circumstances, have children.

But again, I want to reiterate that even a measure as small as procreative licenses will never get off the ground until the issue of procreation is reframed as a privilege instead of a right. As long as adults feel entitled to exploiting children's existence and well-being, they will have no motivation to consider the impact of their actions.

One major argument which is always used against any attempt to change any institution or policy is the "bad apples" rhetoric. Even now this argument is used to shore up the rotten family system: spanking and other forms of "discipline" are only a problem because of a few bad parents, and if only we could stop those few bad parents, there would be no problem with "discipline" at all.

Likewise, there's no doubt that the prospect, or even the specter, of procreative licenses would invoke the same argument. Sure, there's a few people out there who don't "deserve" children (insert veiled classist or racist insults here), but we just need to weed those few bad apples out of the bunch. Most people still "deserve" children.

This is a powerful argument because the vast majority of people are either parents or want to be parents, and they don't want to be called "undeserving." Of course, the issue has nothing to do with being "deserving." No doubt there are people who "deserve" children, but who should not have any. There may also be "undeserving" people who would be allowed to have children under a licensing scheme. The point of such a scheme would not be to measure how "deserving" someone is, but someone's potential ability to raise a child without major fuck-ups that would affect that child's well-being and freedom.

Any limits on procreation must be accompanied by easy and free access to contraception for both sexes, as well as easy and free access to abortion, otherwise it is just another burden on women. In that spirit, I would also propose that, for every instance of a woman having to get an abortion because she doesn't have a license, the man who impregnated her should receive some punishment for being a cause of this hardship. It is men, by and large, who refuse to use contraception, not women. Therefore the men who should be held accountable, not just the women.

I discuss such measures as part of a program of growth reduction, not as antinatalist policies. From the antinatalist perspective, no procreation is acceptable, but most people would never accept antinatalism as true, even if it was true (which I contend it is). But those people may be convinced by antinatalist arguments that some narrow band of procreation is wrong, which is a move in the right direction. Others may adopt views sympathetic to, for example, negative population growth ideas or environmental protection, which is even better.

As I've already said, people will not simply stop procreating. Even if a majority of people became antinatalist or sympathetic to antinatalist ideas, there will always be new people. Realistically, if there was such a movement, it should concentrate, not just on minimizing the number of new births, but also on minimizing the harm that new lives will be exposed to.

But no matter what measures are taken, the only permanent way to reduce harm is to lower the population, and keep lowering it. Everything else will necessarily be overtaken by population growth. So while it is crucial to be concerned with children's rights, women's rights, the environment, abortion, contraception, and similar issues, the bottom line is that procreation itself is wrong and that continuing our current course of procreation can only lead to massive suffering on a scale we've never seen before.

FOOTNOTES

[1] As of the writing of this book, de Giraud has not yet released an English translation, and all quotes from his book are translated by me.

[2] To be clear, I do not believe that evolutionary psychology presents a reasonable portrait of human action, or that it is scientific at all. I recommend to readers who want to learn more on the topic to read Neo-Liberal Genetics, by Susan McKinnon.

[3] My personal position is that some form of ethical intuitionism must be correct, but this is beyond the scope of this book. For more on the subject, I recommend the book Ethical Intuitionism, by Michael Huemer.

[4] Which is not to say that I support cultural relativism. To acknowledge that no individual should be able to impose their values on others does not imply anything about cultures.

[5] For more on that subject, I recommend Delusions of Gender, by Cordelia Fine.

[6] Historical Christianity is a prime example of this, combining extreme homophobia, the push for procreation, and hatred of the body and sexuality, especially hatred of female sexuality.

[7] A conservative once confided in me: "The majority of humans are scum when it gets right down to it. Stupid. Lazy. Evil." No doubt this explains a lot about conservatives.

[8] All quotes by or about A.S. Neill are taken from his book Summerhill School.

[9] Thanks to Sue Lyle for this wonderful find.

[10] Kennedy, D. (2006) The Well of Being: Childhood, Subjectivity, And Education (Suny

Series, Early Childhood Education: Inquiries and Insights) New York: State University of New York Press

[11] For more on the morality of babies, see Why We Cooperate, by Michael Tomasello.

[12] Policy issues are beyond the scope of this book, but on the myths of natalism and possible childfreedom-friendly policies, I would recommend The Baby Matrix, by Laura Carroll.

[13] I actually don't believe that the concept of ownership can apply to human beings, but that's a topic beyond the scope of this book.

[14] On the differential treatment of female students and students of color, see for example:

Fennema E. 1980. Teachers and sex bias in mathematics. Math Teach. 73(3):169-173.

Gunderson EA, Ramirez G, Levine SC, Beilock SL. 2012. The role of Parents and Teachers in the Development of Gender-Related Math Attitudes. Sex Roles. 66(3):153-166.

Townsend BL. 2000. The Disproportionate Discipline of African American Learners: Reducing School Suspensions and Expulsions. Exceptional Children. 66(3):381-391.

[15] For a logical proof of the is/ought gap, see Ethical Intuitionism by Michael Huemer, p. 79-81.

[16] Meta-moral positions are positions about the origin and justification of moral principles. Popular meta-moral positions include divine command theory (an action is good if God says it's good), utilitarianism (actions are good when they bring about the greatest good for the greatest number of people), and cultural relativism (an action is good if your culture promotes it).

[17] For more discussion of child-hatred from ancient times to the present, see for example the works of Lloyd deMause.

[18] See for example Debating Procreation, by David Benatar and David Wasserman, Every Cradle is a Grave, by Sarah Perry, and Confessions of an Antinatalist, by Jim Crawford.

[19] For more discussion of what Benatar calls the "distributional considerations" of suffering and pleasure in a lifetime, see Better Never to Have Been, p61-64.

[20] See Munk-Olsen T. et al., Induced First-Trimester Abortion and Risk of Mental Disorder, N Engl J Med 2011; 364:332-339.

[21] Some may reply that I'm making this far too complicated, and that recognizing our younger body is enough to confirm that it's the same person as me. But this assumes that continuity of the external appearance of the body is the same as continuity of the self, which is doubtful. There is no logical a priori reason to believe that a singular body must always contain the same self.

[22] Kobau, R., Sniezek, J., Zack, M. M., Lucas, R. E. and Burns, A. (2010), Well-Being Assessment: An Evaluation of Well-Being Scales for Public Health and Population Estimates of Well-Being among US Adults. Applied Psychology: Health and Well-Being, 2: 272–297.

[23] To be logically rigorous, we should write "god or gods," but polytheism having fallen into disrepute and monotheism being the only serious theistic position at the moment, no one really bothers.

[24] For more on the attacks against women's control over procreation during the end of the feudal era

and the transition to capitalism, see Caliban and the Witch, by Silvia Federici.

[25] For discussion of the misogynistic aspects of children's stories, see Woman Hating, by Andrea Dworkin.

Made in the USA
Columbia, SC
02 February 2019